Fake It

More Than
100 SHORTCUTS
Every Woman
Needs to Know

D1275869

Jennifer Byrne

A adamsmedia

Avon, Massachusetts

Published by
Adams Media, a division of F+W Media, Inc.
57 Littlefield Street, Avon, MA 02322. U.S.A.
www.adamsmedia.com

ISBN 10: 1-4405-4109-4
ISBN 13: 978-1-4405-4109-4
eISBN 10: 1-4405-4364-X
eISBN 13: 978-1-4405-4364-7

Printed in the United States of America.

10 9 8 7 6 5 4 3 2 1

Library of Congress Cataloging-in-Publication Data

Byrne, Jennifer.
Fake it / Jennifer Byrne.
pages cm
ISBN 978-1-4405-4109-4 (pbk.) – ISBN 1-4405-4109-4 (pbk.) – ISBN 978-1-
4405-4364-7 (ebook) (print) – ISBN 1-4405-4364-X (ebook) (print)
1. Women–Life skills guides. 2. Home economics–Handbooks, manuals, etc.
I. Title.
HQ1221.B97 2012
305.4–dc23
2012026390

This book is available at quantity discounts for bulk purchases.
For information, please call 1-800-289-0963.

Contents

Chapter Two: *Fitting In with the Crowd* *57*

Chapter Three: *Charming Your Prince* *117*

Chapter Four: *Slipping On the Power Suit* *169*

Introduction

Please bear with me as I utter those "three little words" that no woman *ever* wants to hear: *to-do list*. Ouch! About as romantic as a punch in the armpit, right?

However, these dreaded words are actually more similar to those *other* three little words than you might think. If you're anything like me, you might have noticed that to-do lists and I love yous both begin with a ridiculous burst of optimistic cluelessness, and both end in a sad, messy heap of broken promises and failure. The only difference is that to-do lists usually stick around awhile!

Okay, let's just hope you're not anything like me.

Anyway! Back to you and your to-do list. If you take a good look at it, what do you see? I'm guessing for work alone, you've jotted down a meeting, followed by another meeting to discuss the original meeting, and a third meeting to figure out how you're ever going to catch up on all the work you've neglected by sitting in all these meetings. Then your afternoon is probably packed with your kid's play date, a date night, and some date nut bread to bake for tomorrow's bake sale. Oh, and you mustn't forget that, at some point today, you'll also need to make sure you possess all of the following:

- Beautiful, shiny hair in areas where hair is favorable
- Absolutely no hair in zones where hair is frowned upon
- Flawless skin that looks like you didn't slather a bunch of stuff on it, even though you did
- A positive, worry-free, and sexy personality

It seems that, once again, you've got a full plate on your hands. No, not your breakfast plate (aka 'deskfast' plate), you stress-ate that clean while checking your work e-mails, but you totally got this, right? *Right.*

We all know that a mere twenty-four hours just doesn't cut it, and since you can't create more hours in a day or carpool your kids in a *Back to the Future*–esque DeLorean time machine, you'll need to find something that will help you get out from underneath your neverending to-do list and discover that wonderful concept of free time.

Well, look no further! With more than 100 simple (and guiltless) short-cuts for health and beauty, social interactions, relationships, work, and home life, *Fake It* will quickly become your life preserver when you're drowning in a sea of tasks. From maintaining an immaculate house and liking your in-laws to avoiding a major meltdown at work and graciously bowing out of a bad date, this book will give you the advice you need to get through all of the dilemmas you face throughout your day.

CHAPTER ONE

Taming Your Outer Beast

They say it takes a village to raise a child. Okay, but did you know it also takes a village (and possibly a few Village People) to raise the sagging skin from an aging celebrity's neck? Well, it does. In fact, I've long suspected that for every flawless celebrity body part, there is a massive team of underlings working tirelessly, like chic elves, to fight that body part's natural inclination to look awful. There's probably a whole committee on Renée Zellweger's eyes ("Okay, team! This week we're really going for squint-free and fully open, people!"), an entire corporate structure built around Madonna's frightening arms, and a fully licensed company called Janice Dickinson's Entire Head, Inc. (not to be confused with Janice Dickinson's Career, Inc., which has gone out of business). Also, I'm pretty sure that movie *My Left Foot* was all about how Daniel Day-Lewis and his cosmetics team got that gnarly appendage to look camera-ready.

Celebrities have employees whose sole jobs are to tuck, hoover, squeeze, buff, bronze, polish, inject, straighten, curl, transplant, lift, graft, laser, electrocute, and tease until the essential body parts are tormented into looking normal, even pleasant.

This, of course, puts those of us without unionized butt or abs workers at a distinct disadvantage. We sit in front of our lonely TVs and think that if *we just tried harder*—exfoliated more vigorously, did hotter yoga, or purged faster—we might be able to coax all of our poor, tired parts to look decent at the same time. All of this, while actually cleaning our own houses? Please!

So, consider this section a strategic plan for each of your uncooperative body parts, courtesy of the industrious village of Faketown, USA. You might not want to live here, but it's a helpful place to visit!

Clean Hair When Finding Time for a Shower Is Impossible

Ugh, the burdensome task of washing your hair! The last time you tried to do it, it literally took all night. If only you didn't have to lather/rinse/repeat in that horrible endless cycle until your fingertips were chafed raw and you'd used up a jumbo-sized bottle of shampoo. You were hoping the whole thing would be less depressing if you used the "No More Tears" brand, but you still ended up sobbing into your loofa in despair, clutching your washcloth with bloodied fingers. What a ripoff!

In any case, it's been over a week since you last embarked on that dreaded hair-washing chore, and it's really starting to show. Your hair looks like limp, stringy straw, and is so slick with oil that Red Cross volunteers seem to be rinsing ducks they've rescued from your head (aw, it's so heartwarming once the little ducks are all clean and fuzzy again!).

But don't worry—there's hope! All that oil that looks so gross right now? It's moisturizing your hair like nature's leave-in conditioner—for free. So when you wash it next, all of those people who were calling you "Greased Lightning" will have to step back and bask in the splendor of your shiny, lustrous hair. In the meantime, though, your hair is becoming so slick that it's picking up ladies at bars. You need a fake, fast!

Cover Up

The most obvious solution for dirty hair would be to slap a lid on that stuff: a hat, a bandanna, a dunce cap, whatever. It depends on the situation, obviously, and if you're attending a weekend sporting event outside or it's winter, you've hit the lottery. You can put on a winter hat and be done with it. If it's summer and you're headed to an outdoor date, put on a pretty bandanna or headband. If it's Monday and you have to give a presentation to your bosses, a dunce cap is customary (what, your boss doesn't make you wear one, too?). A braid, an up-do, or even parting your hair in a slightly different place can also make your head look less greasetastic.

Try Going Dry

Dry shampoos or "hair powders" are an excellent way to fake clean hair and stop the oil slick. These products usually come as a powder or a light, quick-drying spray, and you'll need to comb it through your hair evenly. Dry shampoos absorb the oil and create the illusion of fastidious hygiene even as you ponder the idea of offering your hair as an alternate fuel source. One thing to keep in mind is that these products often have a "matte" effect, so your hair might look a bit on the dull side, but of course, *dull* is the opposite of "glistening with oil," right? If you really feel like you need shiny hair for a specific reason, you can look for an additional spray to add shine (some hair powder labels include recommendations for shine products). Or, instead of mattifying, degreasing, and then artificially re-shining your hair, another option at this point would be just to go ahead and wash that mess already. Just saying!

Bang, Bang

If you have or have ever had bangs, you know that the hair that seems to get the greasiest is the hair that hangs right above your eyes. You know—that one horrible lock curving greasily into your sightline, whispering to you of the love it has for your forehead, and the beautiful zits they are going to make together. Although I don't have the statistics on it, I am pretty sure that unwashed bangs significantly increase a woman's chances of going completely and utterly insane. What's great about bangs is you can wash them separately. Just pull the rest of your hair back, do a quick wash of those infringing fringes, and blow-dry them. Make sure to warn the rest of your head that it's next!

Flawless Skin for That Big Night Out

So, one morning, you wake up and your face looks like a Domino's five-topping flaky crust special. You have blackheads, whiteheads, and possibly even redheads (they're so feisty and tempestuous!), oil slicks next to frown lines, and pores so huge you're thinking you might be able to rent them out as apartments (no smoking, pets negotiable). And of course this is the day of your big job interview, your passport photo appointment, and—worst of all—your first date with that promising guy you met at your cousin's wedding.

Take a deep breath. You can fix this. If makeup artists can manage to make Madonna not look like an ancient Komodo dragon, there's hope for you.

Fake, but Don't Cake

An important first step to faking perfect skin is to apply a primer or a moisturizer before applying your concealer. If your skin is not properly moisturized, your concealer and foundation is more likely to cake awkwardly around lines and other flaws, making them stand out even more. And while you love cake, you don't want people putting candles on your face and singing "Happy Birthday." So put on primer or moisturizer, wait a few seconds, and then apply your concealer.

Concealed Weapon

Concealer is definitely your friend, but think of it as being like that friend who drinks one too many rum and Cokes and then starts crying about her unrequited crush and singing Michael Bublé songs before passing out. Less is more. It's best to choose a shade that's one or two shades lighter than your foundation, which should match your skin exactly.

Dab the concealer under your eyes, around your nose, and on any other spots that are red or discolored. Then pat it gently, blending it in so that the discolored areas look brighter. Although this brightening is awesome and you might be tempted to add a ton more, please don't. Try to respect the fact that many people have deep-seated fears of mimes and clowns.

Find Your Foundation

Once you've applied your concealer, most of your faking work is done. In fact, you probably don't need to apply foundation to your entire face, just the areas that need coverage. Your foundation shade should match your natural skin tone as closely as possible, so you don't get those telltale lines of demarcation around your jawline. You should also select a foundation based on your skin type and age. If you're over forty, you should avoid powder foundations in favor of a good liquid. Look for products labeled "mature skin" or something equally horrible—it will look better than it sounds, promise.

Foundation should also be tailored to whether you have dry skin or oily skin. For those of us who suffer from the multiple personality disorder of skin, politely known as "combination skin," the choice can be more confusing. For us, it is difficult to tell from day to day—even moment to moment—whether our skin belongs at the prom or the nursing home. Of course, you can try one of those "smart" foundations specifically made for combination skin (if you're wondering how they know where to moisturize and where to de-oil, it's best not to think too hard about it). If this doesn't work, you can keep two separate foundations for either situation and decide each day if your skin is oilier or drier.

Finally, brush on a light dusting of powder, like fairy dust, and check out the amazing magic you've conjured up. Wow! You look gorgeous, and your skin doesn't resemble pizza or cake. I'd say that entitles you to a slice of each!

A Six-Pack for Your First Trip to the Beach

It's summer again, already—can you even believe it? Who saw that coming?

Actually, maybe it shouldn't be *that* hard to believe, after all these years. I mean, given the fact that you've had decades of summers predictably following springs and preceding falls *every single time*, you'd think you might have caught on by now. But no, like most of us, you're caught totally off-guard by it suddenly going from "maximum-clothing-protected season" to "utter-exposure-and-humiliation season." You have not spent the winter working out. You are the color of Cream of Wheat, your muscle tone is a self-esteem booster for jellyfish, and your muffin top has become an entire bakery. You're going to the beach on a double date with your husband, his friend, and his friend's new girlfriend, a *model*. Ugh. You know there's no time for a crash diet, and realistically speaking, there's probably not enough time to start loving yourself and your womanly curves, either. No, in this kind of pinch, there's nothing to be done but fake a six-pack.

Try a "Fake Abs" T-shirt

You know that saying, "Been there, done that, bought the T-shirt?" Well, this is sort of the same concept, minus the "been there" and "done that" part. You might have seen the "fake six-pack" T-shirts out there—basically, they consist of someone else's ridiculously sculpted abs superimposed over your own torso. Unfortunately, it seems the vast majority of these shirts depict *male* six-pack abs, accompanied by shirtless pecs.

So if you try this approach, you should be prepared to unleash a wave of speculation about your gender with your sculpted man-boobs. You can also expect that your participation in a "wet T-shirt contest" will be particularly confusing.

Shock Treatment

Another rather bizarre lazy woman's approach to six-pack abs is the use of those electric shock "ab belts" that are now on the market. These items hearken back to old school "vibration belts" and also to early twentieth-century torture devices. The concept is that by electrically shocking your ab muscles, the muscles will be forced to "work out" by flexing involuntarily. Just flip the switch that conducts the current, and . . . it lives! It tones! Aw, I'm going to call you Flexenstein!

Seriously though, as great as shocking the crapola out of yourself so you don't have to do sit-ups sounds, it's not so certain that these things actually work. In fact, the FTC seems to have clamped down on a few of these products, citing "false claims" by the manufacturers. As it turns out, these things might be more useful in rendering *Jackass*- type stunts on YouTube than in providing you with a valid six-pack. Hmm, so self-electrocution isn't a valid replacement for diet and exercise? Shocker!

Ab Makeover

Probably the best approach to producing faux six-pack abs is also the easiest—just give your stomach a makeover. Elessa Jade of *www.purse buzz.com*, in her *www.youtube.com* video, says you can use makeup to produce subtle, humiliation-sparing abs for that first terrifying beach venture.

Start with a color of foundation that is just slightly darker than your regular skin color. Blend it with sunscreen and rub it in evenly. Then take some mineral powder that's a shade darker than the foundation, and use it to shade in some sculpted areas where a six-pack would be. Don't overdo it, or people might wonder if you've been stabbed. Finally, dust over the whole area with some bronzy powder to produce a shimmery glow.

This approach is mostly intended to jump-start your confidence for beach season since it's going to wash off pretty quickly. But after a day in the sun, you might have some natural color to improve the so-called "situation." Or even better, maybe you won't even care, because you're having such a great time. Or best of all, your friend's gal—the model—turns out to be a *hand* model and is otherwise built just like a normal person.

You totally should have gotten a *manicure!*

A Tan after Your Week-Long Cruise Leaves You Just as Pale as When You Left

You went on that week-long cruise to truly unplug, relax, and get in touch with a calmer, more centered, more in-the-moment you. Well, that, and to make all your friends weep with sickening, office-bound envy over your absolutely flawless tan. Seriously, your plan was to come home such a gorgeous shade of bronze that you ran the risk of being handed out by the International Olympic Committee to a third-place slalom skier. (Hey, he's cute! Nothing wrong with being *his* consolation prize!)

The problem? When it wasn't raining torrentially, you were stuck inside your cabin praying for the end to all tidal motion. Your unexpected bout with seasickness earned you the nickname "Dramamine Queen," and you spent days ejecting your all-inclusive meals from your digestive system, which turned out to be rather all-exclusive. Not only are you not gorgeously tan upon arriving home, you're nuclear meltdown green. And as that wise sage, Jenni "J-Woww" Farley once said, "If you're pale, you fail." What do you do now?

Photoshopping Spree

If it's bragging rights you're after, all you really need is a computer and some basic Photoshop skills to edit your tan after the fact. Just Google "Photoshop tan," and you'll find various tutorials on how to transform your nauseous green memories into gorgeous, sun-kissed do-overs. You can proudly e-mail these pictures to everyone you know, who will coo the expected, "You're *so* lucky!" and "You look *awesome!*" comments you were angling for. The catch? You're going to have to avoid these people for a while. Actually, this isn't that bad since your absence will only add to your exotic mystique. You'll be like everyone's elusive, golden-skinned friend—a tan unicorn.

Lotions and Potions

Of course, you may decide that you actually want to interact with some human beings during the time you're faking this tan. One alternative is to use a sunless tanning lotion or gel. The good news is that you *can* do this without ending up more streaked with rust than a janitorially neglected rest stop urinal.

One trick to achieving the perfect sunless tan is to choose a level of tan that is appropriate to your natural skin color. For example, if you have naturally olive skin, you can go ahead and try products that promote a "deep" or "dark" tan. However, if you are pale as a ghost, the infusion of product on that porcelain white base will make you look like Grandma's yam and marshmallow casserole.

Another modern advantage for us fakers is the invention of tinted self-tanners. These tints will enable you to detect where the product has been applied on your body, sort of like those phosphorescent lights they use on *CSI* to illuminate creepy residue on hotel beds. If you know where the stuff has been slathered, you can avoid overdoing it. *Just* like with hotel beds!

Another important tip to remember is to exfoliate before applying self-tanner. According to writers at *www.ivillage.com*, self-tanners lock onto the top layer of skin and dye it. So if your top layer happens to be rough and scaly, your result will be great—if you want to look like a goldfish. If not, it's very important to take time to slough off any dead or flaky skin before you proceed.

Spray Away!

By now, even that crazy crew from the *Jersey Shore* has abandoned their excessive tanning bed habit for the safer practice of excessive spray tanning. Yes, their skin still looks pretty much like orange rinds picked through by seagulls on the boardwalk. And no, I wouldn't advise taking your fashion cues from people whose oversprayed Bump-its could put someone's eye out. But the key is moderation. You don't have to go so flagrantly orange that student drivers steer carefully around you!

Before you go for your appointment, Susie Hatton, owner of Chocolate Sun Studio, in an interview for *www.allure.com*, recommends that you prepare by exfoliating. You should also wait eight hours after a spray tan to let your skin get wet and also to avoid exfoliating and leg shaving for about a week. Hmm, so maybe you *won't* want to be seeing people after all!

Short Hair When You're Afraid to Commit to Cutting

You've always had a textbook case of what I will call cut-o-phobia. "Cut-o-phobia? Hmm, that actually sounds like the opposite of a problem," you might say, as you sneakily pick up the phone to call the mental health clinic on me. Okay, while I agree that a healthy fear of "cutting" is a super good thing in most cases, it's less awesome when it comes to the technically dead stuff that grows out of our heads. When it comes to hair, fear of making that commitment to a pair of scissors can lead to a chronic case of style blahs.

It's not that you haven't flirted with new styles—you've flirted shamelessly. So shamelessly, in fact, that you've become infamous among hairstylists as a "lock-tease."

Meanwhile, your fear of a commitment has actually *become* a commitment. You've stayed with your current hairstyle for so long that it is technically now your common-law spouse. You've stuck with it through thick and thin (mostly thin—and totally stringy!), and now you're feeling the seven-year itch. Although, actually? That might be dandruff.

If you're not ready to break up with your current style, you can always have a "hair affair." Allow yourself a dalliance with another style—you might fall in love. Or you might find out that the new hair is really grouchy in the morning, snores, and likes to force you to cheer for its favorite football team. Ick.

Wig Out

The most straightforward way to get a short "do" while still maintaining your policy of "don't" is to get yourself a wig. For people who might not have a friendly neighborhood wig shop right next to the five-and-dime and the soda jerk, there's this awesome thing called the world wide web. Some websites even sell custom celebrity-style wigs, so you can basically "scalp" the hairstyles of Reese Witherspoon, Gisele Bündchen, Alicia Keys, and more (no celebrities were harmed in the making of these wigs). These real hair wigs can get fairly pricey, though, so you might want to try some of that synthetic stuff that they sell at the Halloween store. You could theoretically get a used human hair wig at a thrift store, but here I have to ask you: Has it really come down to double-recycled human hair? Would you maybe be better off getting that hair cut than to buy human hair that has been used not once (by the original owner), but twice (by the owner and whoever resold the wig to the shop?) Do you want that much history on your head?

Pin-Up Girl

You're not the only cut-o-phobe out there—you share your hair "wussiness" with lots of celebrities, models, and fashion designers. Just when you think your favorite celeb has chopped off her locks, you discover that it was an ingenious illusion created by those magician hairstylists. Then you learn that it's as simple as a few bobby pins, an elastic band, and opposable thumbs. Emily Hebert at *www.elle.com* says you can create a faux "asymmetrical pixie" by creating a deep side part, pulling hair back, and fastening it in the back, allowing a few strands to show for a casually "mussed" look.

You've also probably heard of the Faux Bob—it's not just my imaginary boyfriend anymore! Celebrities like Rosario Dawson, Kate Beckinsale and Eva Longoria have all been seen sporting the scissor-less bob around Hollywood. According to Dawn Davis at *www.cosmopolitan.com*, you can get this look by pulling your hair into a low, loose ponytail, securing it with a band that matches your hair color, and tucking and pinning it in place with (many) bobby pins. This style works best as a tousled/casual look with wavy hair since "day-old," unwashed hair is more moldable. This is an awesome fakery technique for those of you who eschew shampoo! (See: "Clean Hair When Finding Time for a Shower Is Impossible.") Check it out, you little greasers!

Looking Thin in Pictures

Imagine this scenario: You attend a friend or family member's wedding, and you have an awesome time. You wear "That Dress"—the one that never fails you, the one that makes you feel like a movie star. Your hair is perfect, you radiate confidence, and you charm and dazzle strangers and old acquaintances alike. What a night.

A week later, one of the bridesmaids graciously posts pictures of the wedding on Facebook. They're fine, except you have one question: "Who is the bloated, multi-chinned toad that's wearing your dress?"

For those of us who aren't particularly photogenic, photos can really ruin a good time after the fact. It's like being Cinderella at the ball, and then at midnight having a horrible iPhone photo taken that transforms your head into a giant, misshapen pumpkin.

If this has happened to you, know that you're not alone. Photos capture just a millisecond in time, and if your mouth is twisted the wrong way, your chin clones itself, or your arms are squished unflatteringly at your sides, that millisecond could produce years of embarrassment.

If it makes you feel better, you probably *did* look gorgeous that night. According to Yael Kohen at *www.marieclaire.com*, how you look in photos is all about how light bounces off your face (that's right—"bouncing lights" are the new "big bones"—pass it on).

But because you don't want to be iPhone Cinderella forever, let's discuss fakes for your next photo op.

Spread Your Wings

It is possible that for this occasion, you are wearing a short-sleeved or sleeveless dress. If so, make a point to hold your arms slightly away from your body to avoid what I will delicately call "arm mash." The principle is that sometimes, when you hold your arms too close to your sides, the upper arms flatten and spread against the sides, leading your flesh to look like dough that's imploded in the oven. It's very similar to the "thigh mash" that occurs when you sit down. For that reason, you might want to avoid sitting down, too, if possible. Basically, you should focus on keeping all four limbs from pressing against anything at all, even if you're posing for a picture with Brad Pitt. Sure, he's hot, but when it comes to photos, he's just a surface that will mash your fat. Why do you think Angelina sticks her leg way out there where nothing can touch it?

Strike the Pose

When you were a kid, all you knew about posing for a picture was that it was fun to make rabbit ears behind your sister's head. Today, you still make rabbit ears, just because they're the only part of you that looks thin in a photograph. (Wow, what a svelte rabbit! How *do* you do it?)

But here's the good news: You don't need to resort to weird rodent impressions to look thin anymore! There is a secret pose that women in the know have been using for years to slim their photo images. According to Kohen, the pose involves turning your lower body at a three-quarter angle and putting one hand on your hip. It might seem like a ridiculously sassy way to stand, but just imagine you are getting ready for a gunfight at high noon with Paris Hilton. Supposedly this pose really works, so maybe after you see its results once, you won't feel like a fool doing it the next time.

Chin Up

Quite possibly the fastest way to look heavier than you are in a picture is to accidentally create the photo double chin. This instantly adds both age and weight, and causes the party host to wonder where the extra balloon came from. Don't worry—there is a fairly easy fix. According to *www .bellasugar.com*, you should stand up straight, pull your shoulders back, and stick your chin out about an inch. This won't feel even remotely natural, but do it anyway. Who needs "natural" when you know how to fake it?

Hair-Free Legs When You're Feeling Lazy but Still Want to Wear a Dress

You've been invited to a party in March, that schizophrenic month that can't quite seem to decide whether it wants to be winter or spring. In your lazy world, though, it's still winter. Your legs, especially, have not gotten the memo that spring is approaching. In fact, looking at them, you might think it's the dead of winter in the Antarctic ice sheet.

Of course, the day of the party dawns bright, sunny, and with temperatures expected in the high 70s. You have an adorable sundress that would be perfect for this event, if only your legs weren't insulated with several coats of winter fur. They say March comes in like a lion and goes out like a lamb—I'd say you're going out like a lamb, my friend. A very woolly, woolly lamb.

Okay, you're a lazy shaver. No surprise there. Show me a woman who keeps her legs shiny and smooth all winter long, and I'll show you Richard Simmons. But moving into tricky months like March, lazy shavers need to have a contingency plan in place for unseasonably warm days. Unless you want to claim you're wearing leg warmers.

Hose It Down

You vaguely remember nude pantyhose, right? Those weird things that hatched like aliens out of silver eggs in the '70s and '80s, and made your mom's legs look unnervingly tan and shiny? Those things that bank robbers wore to make their faces all squishy and indistinguishable? "But those are way out of style," you might say. Well, you're wrong. I happen to know that bank robbers still totally *love* nude pantyhose.

Actually, pantyhose have seen a surprising comeback, thanks to the Duchess of Cambridge, Catherine Middleton. Kate has been seen flashing shiny nylon gams all over Buckingham Palace, causing people to wonder if sheer hose are actually back. In reality, she's wearing the nudes not as a fashion statement, but merely in compliance with royal family prudery, which insists that women cloak all shameful below-the-waist appendages. The point is, if you have just a *slight* shadow of stubble, nude hose could provide coverage while still maintaining the look of "bare" legs. If nothing else, the fact that you're actually wearing nude hose will take attention away from the fact that you have hairy legs. And then you can go rob a bank!

The Messy Options

If you know that the quick-fix nude hose approach isn't going to cut it (pun intended) for your leg hair, you have a decision to make. The decision is: Are you more comfortable with pain or mess? Because most of your remaining nonshaving options generally involve one or the other. Based on the fact that you're obviously a bit lazy, I would guess that you're more comfortable with mess, but I don't want to presume. Maybe you're one of those rare lazy neat freaks who would rather suffer than deal with a bunch of glop and goo.

But if you're a pain wuss who's cool with gunk, creams and sprays are your best options.

Yes, they're a mess, and in almost all cases they smell awful. But it's probably better to be known as "smelly chemical legs" than "hairy legs." Right?

The Painful Options

For those of you with more of a "rip off the Band-Aid" psychology, you have many options of the slightly-uncomfortable-but-longer-lasting variety. There are epilators, which consist of a million little electric springs or tweezers yanking your hairs out from the roots. There's waxing, which involves slathering wax on your hairy legs and wrenching them out at the count of three. There's electrolysis and laser, which literally murder your hair.

In addition, there are many products sold for home use that claim to provide "painless" and "permanent" hair removal. They can be found everywhere from Sephora to As Seen On TV websites. Keep in mind, though, that electrolysis is currently the only method the FDA calls permanent. This is because it kills your hair follicles with a jolt of electricity for the crime of producing dark, manly hairs. Finally, justice is done!

Designer Style When You're on a Budget

Everyone knows that girl at work—the one who's always flaunting the hottest new style on the *very same day* it appears in *Vogue Italia*. Sometimes, she's even strutting around the office in the latest trend *before Vogue Italia* has it, like some freakish fashion horoscope. If you didn't know better, you would think she (a) is a billionaire or (b) frequently hides out in the trunks at trunk shows. But no, she spends her days in the cubicle next to yours with her sad little sandwich, so how rich could she possibly be?

Of course, you hate this girl a little bit, but you want to stay on her good side because you suspect she might be from the future. There's so much you *should* want to know from this emissary from the next era—"Will you get that promotion? How many kids will you have? Will world peace ever become a reality?" But instead, all you really want to know is, "How long will this hot pink jeggings craze last?"

This girl is an expert fashion faker. Let's reveal her secrets so she will no longer have such power over you.

Toe the Line

One of the cheapest ways to stay fashion forward is to know what toe is in this season. You know what I mean—last season it was round toes, the season before that it was square toes, next season it will be pointy toes. This toe tyranny is part of what makes the world of fashion go 'round, and you don't have to spend a ton to follow its commands. Just look around, observe what kind of toe is in, and buy a nice pair or two at Target or T. J. Maxx.

Be a Student of Fashion

Another important aspect of being a designer diva is being able to answer the question, "Who are you wearing?" as if you have an actual human being strapped to your back. (Ideally, if you had to have someone strapped to your back, it would be Ryan Gosling, not Badgley or Mischka.)

It's good to know these names, so that you can hunt them down at outlet stores, websites, or thrift stores. Fashion blogs have now become an excellent resource for finding the hottest designers and trends. Take particular note of accessories. Are big belts in? Is it all about hats? Accessories are a cheap, easy way to update a dull outfit.

Also thanks to the Internet, you can now eavesdrop on Fashion Week runway shows without having to change out of your (gasp!) old school tight-ankled sweatpants. Remember, though, that a lot of the outrageous stuff you see on the catwalk is not meant to actually wear, silly. Runway couture is kind of like an expensive joke, like the gag reel in fashion's DVD release. So unless your name starts with Ga and ends with Ga, I would avoid wearing that sleeping bag with mannequin legs sticking out of it to your friend's wedding. Those plastic legs could lure the groom away, and then what?

Don't Be a Trend Slave

Of course, being aware of trends in high fashion is part of what sets a fashionista apart from the Softer Side of Sears. Being in the know, however, is not the same as jumping on every single fleeting trend like it's the last train out of Tackyville. In fact, being too much of a "trend whore" can lead to all kinds of ridiculous fashion mash-ups and mishaps. Remember that girl whose combination of gaucho pants and a poncho made her look so much like a tent that Jake Gyllenhaal and Heath Ledger set her up on Brokeback Mountain? (Actually, that sounds kind of awesome. Bad example). Or the woman, who, upon asking her boyfriend for a "romper" and "shooties" for Christmas, found herself not only minus a man, but involuntarily re-enrolled in preschool? The point is, not every trend is flattering or worth your attention. Particularly if you're on a budget, you don't want to squander what you have on those hot pink jeggings unless you think they will last.

Longer Hair When Summer Rolls Around

Ah, summer! It's a wonderful, easy-breezy, open-toed-shoes-and-bare-legs-under-a-skirt time of year. It's the one time when fashion is as laid back and as comfortable as it's going to get. Still, though, that illusion of comfortable casualness requires rigorous work, maintenance, and the discipline of a Navy SEAL. Let's go down a list. Fake "nature girl" tan? Check. Fake minimalist "Oh, I forgot I was even wearing makeup" makeup? Check. Fake "Oh, tights are just *so* restricting" smooth legs? Check! Fake "I don't even need a bra with this super casual tank top" strapless gravity defying support? Check!

So you're all set to go! Of course, I'm assuming you also have the long, lusciously tousled hair that is best suited to blowing in the breeze as you walk in slow motion down the beach or ride in a convertible. You would never forget that, would you? Surely, you've been growing your "beach hair" all winter like we discussed. Right?

Right?

Okay. When was the last time you saw a movie where the gorgeous girl on the beach was totally unaffected by the sea breeze due to her close-cropped, super-sculpted helmet of hair? Right. Never. In fact, I just Googled "short hair, beach" and one of the first hits was for "British shorthair kittens for sale in Virginia Beach." So if you're a British shorthair kitten, go ahead and strut your adorable self down the beach. For the rest of you, get some hair, already!

Clip It

Faking longer hair has never been easier. Once upon a time, people had to resort to Elvira wigs or those Rasta hats with the fake dreadlocks. Now, you can easily get clip-on hair extensions. In some states, these can be found right in local drugstores or online for the truly lazy girl. You can also check beauty supply stores. Some of these are decent quality and can add length or volume. Jessica Simpson currently sells a line of clip-on hair extensions, which, if all goes well for her, will extend her fifteen minutes of fame as well as your hair. These products take about five minutes to clip on.

If you're up for a more adventurous type of hair extension, there are also feather extensions. These are multicolored feathers from various types of birds that you can stick in your hair, either as clip-ons or in a salon. Note: These feather extensions don't really count as "faking it," unless you plan on pretending you suddenly one day started sprouting feathers like Natalie Portman in *Black Swan*. Trust me, this is not a lifestyle that is very beach- or convertible-friendly.

Pro Job

Professional hair extensions are also much easier—and much higher quality—than they used to be. They are still a bit of a commitment, though, and are more time-consuming and costly. One advantage is that when you're tossing that windswept hair around on the beach in front of admiring eyes, it's less likely to fall off your head and blow into the lifeguard's face if it's a professional job. These extensions are often either sewn or glued onto your natural hair and "grow out" after about four to six months.

Believe it or not, the feather extensions can also be salon attached, in the event that you predict you will want feathers growing from your head for the foreseeable future. If you are still thinking to yourself, "Wait. I still have some disposable income that I'm not wasting on something totally ridiculous," you can also get feather extensions for your *dog*. That's right. You know little Sassy has been getting bored sitting in your purse all day, and the one thing she needs is to have rooster feathers implanted onto her fur for no conceivable reason. That way, when the two of you are walking down the beach, she won't totally humiliate you.

Fuller Lips When You Can't Afford Injections

Oh, that Angelina Jolie—in addition to stealing a man from America's Sweetheart, she also had to go and have those amazing lips without having to have been punctured by needles (which she obviously doesn't mind, anyway!). You know they're natural, too, because you've obsessively tracked them, year after year, looking for any hint of deflation, imperfection or the excess ballooning of an inject-a-holic (you know what I'm talking about, Meg Ryan!). But nope, season after season, year after year, her lips are totally the same, just as though she was actually *born with them*. So unfair! It's like 90 percent of her body weight comes from her lips. (The other 10 percent, presumably, comes from the six kids she's lugging around). Some days, you'd just like to kick those lips like an overinflated tire. But then you'd be thrown into prison in Darfur or wherever you had to go to track her down. Why bother, especially when you can fake full lips on your own meager budget?

Get Stung

One approach to getting those bee-stung lips is to actually go out and get stung by a bee. Believe it or not, this might take some doing. Your first step is to lure the bee by coating your lips with something sugary, such as snow cone syrup, soda pop, or ice cream. (Contrary to the saying, you don't necessarily catch more bees with honey. I mean, *think* about it: They have their own supply.) If you're in doubt, just coat your lips with whatever your kids are eating. That ought to do it.

Once the bee is hovering around your lips, the next step is to convince it to sting you. You might need to physically threaten it, but this is tricky, because you don't want to kill it. My personal advice is to call it names, insult its mother, or imply that those horizontal stripes aren't doing it any favors. If that doesn't work, appeal to its sense of pity, tell it about Angelina, and see if it decides to have mercy on you. Make sure it isn't a wasp first—wasp-stung lips aren't so fabulous at all.

Draw the Line

A much more practical—and safe—approach to getting fuller lips is to use lip liner. According to a contributor at *www.ehow.com*, lip liner is a painless, inexpensive way to create the illusion of significantly fuller lips. Start by applying concealer or foundation to your lips, making sure you blend it in well. Then use your lip liner, which should be close to the natural color of your lips, to line the outermost edges of your lips. Color in the inside of your lips with the liner, blending the color as you go. Finally, apply a clear or natural-colored gloss or plumper (see "Plump It") to complete the look. Remember, your lines should not be ridiculously outside the natural lip line, unless you want to look like you're sporting those giant wax-candy lips.

Plump It

You've probably heard about "lip plumpers," which temporarily produce injection-free, Jolie-like swelling of the lips. There are many of these currently on the market, and they can be found in any old drug store. According to Sarah Siddons at *http://health.howstuffworks.com*, plumpers are based on the principle of irritation (no, this doesn't mean you can get fuller lips just by talking to your annoying ex or your difficult boss). Plumpers use mildly irritating ingredients, which cause a "stinging" effect, causing increased blood flow and swelling. Some of the common household ingredients used for this effect are ginger, peppermint oil, cayenne pepper, cinnamon, and menthol. So if you don't want to buy a plumper at the store, you can make your own using these ingredients. Make sure you're not allergic to any of these items, though—anaphylactic shock lips are *so* last year!

A Bigger Butt When You Want to Look Good in Your New Jeans

Kids, pull up a chair, I'm going to tell you a little story. Once upon a time, having a big butt was *not* the most awesome thing around. In this time long, long ago, ladies actually worked very, very hard to make their butts *smaller*. They worked out on torture contraptions, they paid a small fortune for liposuction, and they starved themselves to within an inch of their lives to make their butts the tiniest bit tinier. Only one courageous and valiant knight, whose name was Sir Mix-A-Lot, stood up in defense of the lusciousness of the big booty. Sir Lot was as honest as he was honorable and had to admit that he liked big butts and he simply could not lie about this.

Then there came a famous family called the Kardashians. "Were they movie stars?" you ask. "Singers? Artists?" Hey, don't worry about that. That's not the point. They were cute, and their names all started with K! Isn't that enough for you?

One of these young ladies became extra famous for having a plentiful booty, setting off a big-butt craze that left many of us small-butt seekers baffled but relieved. When rumors surfaced that the junk in her trunk was *fake*, all the skinny women knew they needed to copy that look. As for the ample-butted women? We knew this was a sign of the end of the world, and it made us hungry.

Eat Some Food

For pear-shaped types, acquiring a bigger butt is just the easiest thing ever. All we have to do is eat some food. Instead of the usual starvation salad at lunch, try a sandwich. It doesn't need to be a huge sandwich, just one with a carb or two, and you will begin to see results almost right away. For dinner, once again, try eating. No need to gorge, just eat a reasonable, well-balanced meal that leaves your stomach not growling, and this nutrition will magically go straight to your butt. How does it know where to go? We can't say. It's truly a mystery. However, if you're looking to be booty-licious in those new jeans, don't overdo it. Awesome buns are great; muffin tops are not. Know which bakery items you want in your pants!

Lose Weight

Before I begin to sound like a total hypocrite (I am, but that's beside the point), this next tip is for apple-shaped ladies only. Women who naturally collect weight in your butts may happily disregard this as you chomp down on a sandwich.

For women who tend to gain weight in your stomachs or arms, losing a little bit of weight will actually help create the appearance of a bigger butt. If your upper body is naturally bigger than your lower body, it stands to reason that your booty will be underwhelming in comparison to your belly. And really, no one wants a big stomach or chunky arms, anyway. So all you have to do is lose some weight from your upper body, and hopefully, your butt will stand out even when you sit down.

Fake Your Cakes!!

If you happen to be a person who can't pack on the booty just by thinking about food, or if you accidentally lost your caboose like a derailed train, it's still totally possible to get some junk into that trunk! These days, there are a wide variety of temporary "fake cakes" for sale. Silicone butt shapers, padded panties, and various similar products give your booty lift as well as volume to achieve that round, sexy butt that is so sought after. It's like those old-fashioned "falsies" our moms and grandmothers put in their bras, only now the padding is in the seat. There are even swim-suits available with top and bottom padding. Awesome! Can normal-sized supermodels be far behind?

Killer Legs When It's Miniskirt Season

It's miniskirt season, and you have a pair of legs that won't quit. You kind of wish they would quit, though, because you've been seriously thinking of firing them. As legs go, they really don't follow even your most basic instructions, such as, "Be thin, appear several inches longer than you are, stop rubbing up against each other—that's so disgust-ing." You've spoken to the HR department in your head about how best to let these legs go, but you've been advised that due to the whole standing-up-and-helping-you-walk thing, you really do need to keep them on. Sigh. All you can do is suck it up and hope they will give their two weeks' notice.

Sadly, not all of us are naturally blessed with the long, lean legs that miniskirts were created to show off. Some of us just naturally have bigger lower bodies—even when we diet and exercise, we tend to collect weight below the waist. It's what nice people call *pear-shaped,* and what horrible, horrible people call a *genetic fat-suit.*

It's true that legs can be a very stubborn body part, but there are plenty of quick tricks you can use to put on that miniskirt and take the world by storm (not even a thunder thigh storm, either!).

Create a Media Blitz

One way to get killer legs without moving from your couch is to simply redefine the public perception of what killer legs are. I mean, who would have seen the "big-butt" trend coming (even though we'll all watch it as it leaves)? If big butts got to be so popular that women are buying padded panties, who's to say big thighs won't have their day in the sun? The fastest way to popularize chunky legs is to spread a rumor that some celebrity either has or wants them. Start a blog that speculates, "Are so-and-so's huge thighs real, or is she wearing silicone fakes?" Discuss how all the celebs are getting thigh fat injections and cankle implants. Plant the seed, sit back, and watch it grow. Note: This could possibly take a long time, maybe even your whole lifetime. But your grandkids—if you insist on continuing your thigh genetics—will get to walk around in the teeniest of skirts with pride. It's a beautiful legacy (pun intended).

Let the Lymph Flow

You've already tried to get slimmer legs by restricting calories, cutting carbs, eating nothing but cabbage soup, and whatever other deprivation craze came to your attention. And while some of these diets may have helped you lose overall weight, they've never really helped take the thunder out of your thighs. According to Liz Bestick at the *www.telegraph.*

co.uk, a more reasonable dietary change is to eat to maintain lymph flow. The lymphatic system helps flush toxins from your body, and when the lymph is slow or ineffective, it can retain toxins and cause bulkier legs. Foods that slow down lymph flow include caffeine, alcohol, and highly refined items like simple carbs. In addition, there are vitamin supplements, such as diosmin, which are designed to boost circulation. And yeah, exercise doesn't hurt either.

If you were just starting to think this all sounds suspiciously like a straight-up diet-and-exercise program in sheep's clothing, think again. Bestick reports that massage also improves circulation and lymph flow, and can "potentially take inches off thighs in a session." Nice. *Go get a massage right now, so that your legs will be thinner.* That is the kind of command a girl likes to obey.

Larger and Brighter Eyes When You Haven't Slept for Days

Maybe you've been out all night painting the town red, or maybe you've been in all night repainting the walls burnt umber (*Hello*, that house isn't going to remodel itself!). Perhaps you and your amazing new soulmate couldn't bear to fall asleep for even a second (you'd miss each other!), or maybe your four-year-old couldn't bear to resist peeing on his newly changed sheets. Maybe you're a wild bohemian who lives a restless lifestyle, or maybe you have restless leg syndrome. You really should ask your doctor about that.

Whatever your reason, it's been a few days since you've slept, and your eyes are giving you away. They're bloodshot, puffy, and about half their usual size and radiance. If they are, in fact, a window to your soul, your soul is looking like a house on *Hoarders*.

Yet even though your insides are a complete jumble of madness, your outsides look like a very lazy basset hound, and while I'm not sure what your day will demand of you, eye-wise, most daytime activities call for eyes to remain open. You need a fake, and quick!

About Last Night . . .

Okay, we have to face one unfortunate reality—there is such a thing as *good* sleep deprivation vs. *bad* sleep deprivation. It's one thing to be up all night canoodling with your soulmate, Mr. Sexypants, and another to be rehearsing a PowerPoint presentation while changing diapers. It's one thing to be living it up at an awesome New Year's Eve party, and another to be sobbing into your pillow because some jerk gave you the old, "It's not you, it's me," routine.

If you're going to have to miss valuable, brain-regenerating hours of rapid eye movement, it's best to do so for activities you can recall the next morning with a sassy, knowing little smirk. The fact is, *good* sleep loss might cause puffy lids or dark circles, but it also puts a spark of irresistible confidence and vitality into those corneas that money can't buy.

So, here's what I advise. Because you're borderline insane and possibly hallucinogenic anyway, I propose that you "reimagine" your reasons for sleep loss. Edit out the crying baby and pencil in an unforgettable party where *you* were the dancing queen. Blot out the cowardly dumping and replace it with a random, all-night encounter with George Clooney. For one day, lie to yourself utterly. Make it convincing by putting a night-clubbish stamp on your hand, even if it's only your daughter's Strawberry Shortcake stamp. You'll barely know the difference, trust me!

De-Puff

The first thing your eyes will probably need is for you to deflate the puffy, parade-float lids that are stealing the show from your actual eye-balls. According to an article at *www.goodhousekeeping.com*, part of the answer is cold and caffeine. No, I'm not talking about an iced mochaccino, although, what the hell, go ahead and have one of those, too.

Look for an eyelid gel or serum that contains caffeine and peptides, which act to boost collagen while reducing puff. To really maximize that effect, pop these products in the fridge first. You'll find the coolness sooth-ing, and it will also reduce the swelling.

Create an Illusion

Makeup is the single most important tool at your disposal for faking big, bright eyes after serious sleep loss. According to YouTube makeup guru Michelle Phan, there are specific colors and applications that can brighten and open up tired, droopy eyes. Phan suggests starting by lining your lower lids with white eyeliner. Next, apply a light colored eye shadow to your upper lids, and use a silver eye shadow on your upper brow line and near your tear ducts (if you've been crying, wait until you're finished first). If you need to pencil or shade in your eyebrows, do that. Lastly, curl your eyelashes with one of those little torture device-looking things, and then apply mascara, holding a business card behind your upper lashes while applying, so you can get each lash. Hopefully, if you manage to cre-ate the illusion of alert normalcy, this won't be the last time you use your business cards today!

A Manicure When You Don't Have the Time or Funds for One

Lately, you've been such a busy multitasker, you really could use several extra pairs of hands, like that Hindu goddess, what's-her-name. Of course, if you did have several extra pairs of hands, it would only highlight how badly in need of a manicure all of those hands are.

Here you thought you were on top of your beauty priorities—you've been padded, coiffed, reshaped, buffed, and de-puffed. You look like a million bucks, but when you go to shake a client's hand, your value gets slashed to half-price clearance. Look at those hands: dried-up husks of winter skin with cuticles gone wild, chipped polish from two months ago, and a "manicure" administered nervously by your own teeth. Your hands have sold you right down the river.

Can you blame them, really? They've worked so hard for you, balancing work, family, friendships, and romance. You've used them to beautify the rest of your body. And what have you given them? *Maybe* some CVS hand cream—if you remembered.

Sadly, when things get busy, your hands are the first to suffer. Do you really want to be the person who worked this hard to look fabulous, only to drop the ball in the end zone? Hey, why the sudden confusing football metaphor? you might ask. Okay, here's why: If you don't deploy a fake manicure ASAP, you're going to have man-hands.

Get a Job at a Hazmat Facility

One way to avoid having to deal with your unmanicured mitts is to get a job working with noxious chemicals. In this setting, you will be required to wear rubber gloves all day long as you deal with toxic spills and radioactive particles. The gloves will match your giant silver space suit and will protect you against both gaseous contaminants and the humiliation of not having had a manicure in a year. The best part? Your colleagues will be exactly the same as you. When you go to shake hands, it will be rubber gloves shaking rubber gloves. And if, by some chance, your wretched paws are revealed, everyone will assume it was your rough working environment that did it. Either way, you're covered!

Quick Fix

Of course, you might think that a lifetime of exposure to horrible chemicals is a high price to pay for hiding your bad hands. True, but manicures aren't exactly cheap, either.

If you're just about to leave the house and you realize your hands make Edward Scissorhands's hands look neat and well maintained, you need a quick fix. According to editors at *www.dailyglow.com*, you can achieve a beautifully manicured look in about five minutes. First, apply cuticle oil (or baby oil) to the base of your nails, and use a cuticle stick to gently push cuticles back. This creates a neat appearance and makes your nails look a little bit longer. Then buff your nails with a nail buffer, passing it over each nail in only one direction until the nail is smooth. You can then create the shape of your nails with an emery board, again, filing in only one direction. Apply some hand cream, a layer of base coat, and prepare to polish.

Try Dry

There are few things more annoying to you than waiting for nail polish to dry. You can't touch anything, you can't pick anything up, and you're stuck fanning yourself flamboyantly like a character in *Steel Magnolias*. It's all just a little too leisurely for a person whose day planner is fuller than a tick at a blood drive.

If you'd prefer a freshly applied polish job without having to wait around, there's a faster way: dry nail appliqués. According to *www.the beautycult.com*, these are actually dry strips of nail polish that are flexible and can be molded to your nails to create a faux manicure look. You can smooth them out and use a nail file to remove any extra material. Dry polish lasts about two weeks, and the polish can be removed just like any other polish—with nail polish remover. No fanning, no incapacitating wait. How handy!

Beach Hair When You Know You'll Be Stuck Inside All Summer

Hey, indoor girl! Time to face facts: summer is here, even if the closest thing to sunlight you're going to see is the flash of the photocopier. (Tip: Do *not* use the photocopier as a tanning bed, especially for your butt, no matter how often that cute guy in your office dares you to.)

Let me start by consoling you. I'm very sorry that for whatever reason, you're going to be stuck inside this summer. It's really no fun, but hopefully, there's a good reason you're doing it—maybe the work you're doing this summer will make a huge difference to your career, maybe you're holed up in some love nest with Mr. Hunkyfunk (in which case, I take it back, I'm *not* sorry for you), or maybe your top modeling agency has required you to maintain your porcelain skin as part of your multi-million dollar contract. Again, I'm not crying so hard for you.

Beach Hair Psychology

Let me let you in on a little secret about "beach hair": It's an adaptive technique. See, once we women began to understand what soup-thick humidity, chlorine, saltwater, and sea breezes do to hair, we thought, "Shit. This weather is awesome, but this hair really sucks." In the early days, maybe we tried valiantly to wage battle with our straightening irons, our smoothing gels, and our anti-frizz products, only to end each day sadly defeated by summer. Then one day, some brilliant spin artist of a woman came up with a catchall term for the sentiment, "Eff this! I give up on trying to control my hair in the summer." That term? "Beach hair."

Beach hair is a wonderful, beautiful term, because it makes giving up sound fun, casual, and kind of primal. But as an indoor creature, you don't *have* to give up! *Your* hair can still be sleek, smooth, and flawless. Not only will you spend significantly less time out in the frizz-inducing humidity than your sun-worshipping friends, you'll have much less sun damage, dryness, and fewer split ends. Hooray!

The Highlight of Your Summer

Just to be seasonal, though, you might still occasionally want that sought-after beach look, and the first step is to get some sun-kissed color. But just take a minute to think first—do you want to artificially damage your hair even more than you would with the sun? Of course not! There's nothing worse than a bad, streaky bleach job under garish fluorescent lights. So proceed wisely. According to celebrity colorist Eva Scrivo in *www.elle.com*, you might want to avoid the traditional "foil" highlights for two reasons: One, foil highlighting works with four- to five-inch sections of hair at a time, which often results in overhighlighting. Secondly, the foils are a conductor of heat, which is damaging and can cause a "brassy" color. Instead, Scrivo recommends the balayage method of coloring—which I've never heard of either. Basically, this method involves highlighting as much or as little hair as you want, allowing for a more natural result. Remember, if you don't leave some dark in, there's nothing to show the highlights against. If you highlight everything, you're not really highlighting anything. Got it?

Wave Hello

Another component to beach hair, other than lots of sand and the occasional syringe, is gorgeous wave. According to Sarah of West Virginia University writing on *www.collegefashion.net*, most of us have a certain amount of natural wave to our hair, and they suggest bringing this out by *spraying salt in our hair*. Yes, salt, which makes you bloated when you eat it and causes slugs to melt on the sidewalk, is actually a good idea for your summer hair. Specifically, products called "salt sprays" are designed to create those "beachy" waves. Salt sprays can be drying, though, so it's best not to use them every day unless your goal is to look authentically beach-damaged.

For extra wave, you can use a large-barreled curling iron, or braid your hair at night while it's still damp and then sleep on it. Even if the only surfing you do is at your laptop, you're going to have the best beach hair in town!

Bangs When You Aren't Sure If You Can Pull Off the Style

You and bangs—throughout your life, it's been a turbulent, love-hate relationship. The first time you and bangs met, it was the day before second-grade school pictures, when your BFF Kimmy gave you a "bowl cut" in her basement, and she unwisely opted to use that asymmetrical "Picasso Style" bowl her mom made in ceramics. You didn't even have to fake being sick on picture day—you were vomiting out of genuine disgust and horror. And your mom couldn't even hold your hair away from your face—not entirely—because of those cubist bangs of yours.

This set the course for the rest of your life. Even after those bangs grew out, bangs have always prompted a complex mix of longing, hesitation, and outright fear in you. "Should I, or shouldn't I?" is the "big bang" question in your life, and it tends to crop up every few years. Your dream is that your face will be adorably and stylishly transformed. Your nightmare is that you will resemble the *Star Trek* Vulcan Mr. Spock.

Recently, you've had a flare-up of the old itch for bangs. But you're scared that you will end up looking less rockabilly and more Spockabilly.

Relax! You don't have to commit to bangs until you are good and ready. Times have changed. Remember, "Change is the essential process of all existence." I think it was Spock who said that.

Get a Celebrity Face

One excellent, scissor-less way to 100 percent guarantee ahead of time that bangs will look awesome on you is to pretty much transform your face into that of your favorite bang-wearing celebrity. Just grab a *People* or an *US Weekly* magazine and find the adorable, bang-wearing starlet whose picture you would ordinarily cut out and bring to your hairstylist to duplicate. Normally at that point, your stylist, caring and professional individual that he or she is, might warn you, "Your face is really shaped very differently than hers," or, "I can give you her cut, but not her face, of course (chuckle, chuckle)."

Okay, zip it, stylist. This tip is designed to bypass your ass.

Consider this: Instead of taking that magazine picture and going to your hairstylist with it, go directly for the gold and take it to the nearest plastic surgeon.

Instruct the good doctor to do as many painful, costly procedures as necessary to make your face identical to the picture. Once that's been achieved, there can be absolutely no doubt that bangs will look phenomenal on you, since you are now her twin.

This approach might seem rather extreme and invasive, and it's possible that, after blowing your life savings on extensive facial reconstruction, you might not be able to scrape together that last $12.99 for some Hair Cuttery Bangs. Hmm, well, maybe you can check to see if your childhood friend Kimmy is still available?

Make Your Own

If extensive face cutting doesn't seem to you like a great alternative to bang cutting, there are definitely some teeny tiny baby steps you can take, as well. For example, it's pretty easy to make your own temporary bangs using a brush, a headband or hat, and a few bobby pins. Here's a really simple tutorial from YouTube hairstylist BeautyNewbie. Start by making a high, tight "whale spout" ponytail on the top of your head, like it's the '80s and you're desperately trying to look like Debbie Gibson but end up resembling a water fountain. This pony can be arranged to hang down over your forehead like bangs. Lift the hair to the desired length, and then pin down your fake bangs with bobby pins. Use the hat or bandanna to cover the extra hair pinned up on the top of your head.

If you aren't quite skilled enough to manipulate your own hair into bangs, don't worry. You can always buy clip-in bangs. These can be found online, in beauty supply stores, or from stores like Urban Outfitters. Some of these are made with someone else's hair, and some aren't, but all are made with someone else's effort. Lazy girls rejoice!

A Tattoo When You're Not Sure You're Ready for Some Real Ink

Lately, it seems you've become obsessed with the idea of getting a tattoo. Maybe it's the lure of gorgeous celebrities with cool ink, or maybe you've met someone amazing whose name you're just dying to have emblazoned on your body for all time, or maybe you just really love your mom. Whatever your reasons, you've been looking up Chinese characters online, asking tattooed friends to rate the pain from one to ten, and leafing through *The Girl with the Dragon Tattoo* in search of illustrations (there are none—what a ripoff *that* book is).

So what's stopping you? Well, tattoos are just so *permanent,* or at least semi-permanent. How can you be sure you're still going to love this guy Chip when you're eighty years old? (If you get his name on your hip, though, you can pull a Johnny Depp and edit your tattoo to say "hip." You'll look like a textbook anatomy chart, which might help the surgeon who eventually does your hip replacement.) How can you be sure your mom isn't going to seriously annoy you sometime soon? And how can you guarantee that the Chinese character really does translate to "New Beginnings" and not "Kick me, I'm a total American sucker!"?

Get a Hypothetical Tattoo

The first step to faking a tattoo is getting a hypothetical one first, using your imagination. This hypothetical tattoo will serve the purpose of showing you the potential roadblocks and future problems you might have. You can then adjust your life accordingly. For example, if you're dating a guy named David, your only post-breakup editing option would be to change it to "avid." If you do this, you'll have to add something like "birdwatcher," or "doll collector," just so it makes sense, and then take up that hobby. Likewise, if your true love is named "Jonathan" and you're not 100 percent sure of him, you should acquire a good friend named Nathan who is secretly in love with you. Nathan will be an excellent backup in case you catch Jonathan making out with your best friend in the Olive Garden bathroom during your birthday dinner. Not that such a thing has ever happened to anyone I know.

Get a Cereal Box Tattoo

Remember when you were a kid and would get those temporary tattoos out of the bottom of the cereal box or a gumball machine? True, they might have been of the Care Bears or Foghorn Leghorn, but so what? You just put the tattoo on your skin, pressed down with a wet sponge, and voilà! You had a tattoo. These are easy, totally commitment-free alternatives to getting real ink. In fact, they're so commitment-free that if you accidentally rub up against something, or look at them too hard, they might peel right off. What did you expect from a Lucky Charms prize? Seriously, though, classy designers like Chanel now offer their grown-up version of these temporary tattoos. Too bad they don't make a cereal, too!

Make Your Own

If you're more of a DIY type, you can actually create your own temporary tattoo using Sharpies. According to a tutorial from artist MakeupholicLiz, you can create a tattoo using a picture of your desired image, tracing paper, scissors, fine-point Sharpies, a tattoo pencil (sold at craft stores), alcohol-based deodorant, Q-Tips, and 99 percent alcohol. Your first step is to use your tattoo pencil to trace the design onto the tracing paper. Once you've traced the design, carefully cut it out. Next, apply the deodorant onto your skin where you want the tattoo to be. Apply the cutout pencil-side down onto your skin and press down. Peel the paper away carefully.

Next is the fun part—break out the Sharpies! Using a black Sharpie, carefully trace over the outline you did in pencil. Then use your colors to slightly shade—but not fully color in—the inside of your tattoo. Next, put some of the 99 percent alcohol on a Q-Tip, and dab the colored parts to blend. Your ink is beautiful today but will be long gone when you're eighty!

Fuller Eyebrows When You're the Victim of a Botched Waxing Job

You *almost* turned around and left the salon when you heard that your usual eyebrow stylist had called in sick, but it's date night, and you'd really prefer not to respond to your guy's flirty innuendoes by sexily raising your unibrow. So instead of leaving, you agree to have your brows—which have indeed reached Martin Scorsese proportions (and I don't mean "Oscar winning")—pruned by this stranger, whom we'll simply call "Sadistic Torturer Who Obviously Hates You."

"So, we'll just clean these up a little bit?" S. T. W. O. H. Y. asks, as she settles you onto her rack of horror. "Sure," you say. It all sounds perfectly reasonable, doesn't it? Little did you know that "clean these up" was code for "cause you to look like a cross between a flapper and a burn victim." Seriously, the thin, bizarre looking zigzags of hair that were left when she was done resemble the EKG monitor readout of someone who is having a major cardiac event—which is probably what's going to happen to your husband when he sees you.

Pencil It In

For short-term goals, such as not looking like a permanently shocked crazy woman tonight, you need to pick up your pencil and get to work like you're taking the SATs. If you have pale eyebrows, says Jenny Bailly on *www.oprah.com*, you should choose a color that is two shades darker than your natural color, and if your brows are dark, you should choose a color that is two shades lighter. Use the pencil to gently trace along the brows' upper edges, then fill in the inner corners and end with light strokes. Don't press down too hard, and don't ever use black pencil! No one looks sane with overdone, dramatic brows. Bailly also recommends penciling in your eyebrows before you apply your eye makeup. And now, time is up, pencils down. You might just have earned admission into Eyebrow Harvard!

No Pain, No Rogaine

For the longer term, you can take the approach of treating your missing eyebrows like bald men having a midlife crisis. Yep, I'm talking about Rogaine. According to Darla Ferrara at *www.livestrong.com*, Rogaine can be used to treat the eyebrow baldness caused by that heartless waxstress. Ferrara suggests dabbing the Rogaine on with a Q-Tip twice a day. Only put a thin layer on the eyebrows, and be careful to avoid getting it into your eyes (hairy eyeballs are *not* sexy). On the negative side, you may need to use this for up to six months before you start to see results. Oh, and you may also grow a mustache. According to *New York Times* writer Alex Kuczynski in her book, *Beauty Junkies*, the use of Women's Rogaine didn't do much for her eyebrows, but it was very useful in reversing that pesky baldness on her upper lip.

It should also be noted that the company that makes Rogaine does not recommend its use for this purpose. So maybe if your poor eyebrows are really having a midlife crisis, they should handle it like everyone else does: with a new red convertible and some Viagra.

Nutrition and Massage

If you prefer not to treat your eyebrows like they're sad little middle-aged men, you can instead act like they are pampered middle-aged ladies on a spa weekend (minus the discreet overindulgence in apricot bellinis and the not-so-discreet sexual harassment of the male yoga instructor). Heather Topham Wood at *www.livestrong.com* recommends giving your brows a daily massage to stimulate hair growth. You can use a little bit of coconut oil because, well, it smells awesome, and why the hell not. Eating foods high in protein, iron, and B, C, and E vitamins is also helpful in coaxing those brows back into existence.

Finally, you might be able to find "eyebrow conditioner" products, designed to promote brow growth. If you treat your eyebrows like they're valuable and special, they will be very suspicious of your motives, which is excellent because this will cause them to arch quizzically. Beautiful!

A Good Profile Photo on Your Social Networking Page

You've been on that social network created by that infamous nerdy zillionaire (let's call him "Gark Schluckerblerg") for a while now, and the only decent profile picture you've come up with is one depicting your kitten stuck inside a vase. As awesome as kittens stuck inside vases invariably are, after about a year or so of delightful kitten entrapment, your Facebook "friends" started asking questions. These days, your wall comments are pretty much all variations of, "Where's a picture of *you*?" and "Have you turned into a kitten stuck inside a vase??" and "Please let me out of this vase. Love, the kitten."

Seriously, you need to let that kitten out of the vase—that's not nice, especially since it's probably a full-grown cat by now and in a total panic. While baby animals being precociously clumsy is cute, adult creatures in a total panic are less adorable. All anyone needs to do to see adult beings freaking out is go to work, to the DMV, or to Wall Street.

The truth is, you've coasted by on this kitten picture for too long now, and you need to post a decent profile picture of yourself. What's that, you say? You take terrible pictures? Not to worry. Just fake it! There are lots of options for this.

Declare It "Celebrity Look-a-Like Day"

One of the best aspects of social networking is being able to declare any day "celebrity look-a-like day." On these days, you can choose a celebrity you subjectively think you look remotely like, based on the very loosest of criteria. For example: do you have approximately the same number of ears as Scarlett Johansson? Wow, that is uncanny! So post Scar-Jo's picture, and declare it "Celebrity Look-a-Like Day." Don't worry, no one will try to quibble with you on this. Instead, you'll start seeing pics of Megan Fox, Natalie Portman, and Tina Fey (for *Every. Single. Woman.* who wears glasses!) popping up all over your friends' lists. Everyone will happily and gratefully misrepresent themselves as celebrities who are much, much more attractive than they are.

Kid Pictures

Another brilliant profile picture fake is to use pictures of your adorable kids. Granted, it's the same overall approach as the kitten-in-the-vase ploy, but it'll work for much longer because the "kid card" is a very powerful weapon. People intuitively understand that posting pictures of your kids means you are too busy being a mom to worry about such vanities as taking good pictures or looking good or being seen by any human eye ever again. It's not about you anymore; it's about The Kids. You are the saintly behind-the-scenes matriarch dressing Jayden and Sophia up for their professional portraits and their action shots at Bouncy Jounce. It's brilliant; no one will have the nerve to ask what *you* actually look like. You are like an ephemeral spirit hovering above all of the petty nonsense of looking like something.

No Myspace Angles!

Let's address the subject of "Myspace-angle" photos, as well "mirror-cam" pics with the pouty expression and the extended, camera phone-bearing arm. They are awful. Nothing makes a woman seem more simultaneously ridiculous, boring and in need of arm weight reps like these poses do. Those shot-from-above pics scream, "Look! I have cleavage and a working phone! All this can be yours!" They also have now become the official opposite of original.

Instead, Connie Wang at *www.refinery29.com* recommends using "action" photos that depict you doing something interesting, such as climbing a mountain or standing next to (a cardboard cutout of) Johnny Depp. To achieve a flattering pic, seek out soft lighting, such as morning, evening, or clouded light.

If you insist on a "shot-from-above" pose, why not go for the highest, most flattering heights and use a picture from Google Earth? If you have to, you can pin one of those little markers on a mountain range and identify it as "my boobs (trust me, they R *huge*!)" or a tree as "my camera arm (*so* not flabby!). Everyone will be so grateful that your "Myspace angle" left you with a LOT more space!

CHAPTER TWO

Fitting In with the Crowd

We've all been taught to never, ever worry about "fitting in" and to happily let our freak flags fly all over the place. We're supposed to think that standing out like a sore thumb is great, as long as that sore thumb is giving the thumbs up.

There are, however, situations in life where standing out is not necessarily a wonderful thing. Being a fluorescent pink gazelle in the sandy-colored desert, for example, is a great way to win the Most Likely to Be Eaten First award. And being the creep who uses the salad fork instead of the regular dinner fork is a great way to get your handprint on the Dinner Guest Walk of Shame (because you may as well just eat with your hands, you barbarian).

The point is, there are times where standing out from the pack shows integrity and originality—and there are other times when it just shows you didn't have the tact or good sense to fake it. You don't want to be the one person who tells your friend her outfit is three sizes too small, her boyfriend is a jerk, and her cooking is disgusting. (Hopefully this isn't all the same friend—if so, why are you even hanging out with this person?)

Knowing when to make a bold statement and when to blend in is an important skill to have and use throughout life. Knowing *how* to blend in is an awesome way to not be devoured by a mountain lion.

Liking a Crappy Dinner at a Friend's House

A beloved friend of yours invites you and your significant other to come to her house for a dinner prepared by her new guy. It sounds great, until you get there and discover the menu.

Apparently, the new man is something of an "extreme foodie," with a leaning toward exotic (i.e., inedible) food. He must be some sort of wizard in the bedroom because he has hypnotized your friend so completely that she's practically clucking like a chicken. Actually, chicken clucking would be music to your ears right now because it would give you hope that *maybe*, just *maybe*, you might get something normal to eat tonight.

Alas, the chances of that are looking slim. Tonight's menu consists of braised pork knuckles, llama bone marrow, and pickled, deep-fried octopus. The side dish is Brussels sprouts in a maple mustard glaze.

"Don't forget to eat the octopus eyes!" the horrible boyfriend specifies, as your friend nods with a terrifyingly vacant, Stepford-wife smile. "The eyes are the best part!"

Everyone sits down at the table, which would give any episode of *Fear Factor* a genuine run for its money. Now he's dishing out the awfulness and telling you how much you will love it. All eyes are on you—including the octopus's.

Cough It Up

Remember the approach you used to take to gross food when you were a kid? You would put the food in your mouth, pretend to chew it, and then "politely" cover your mouth with a napkin as you started to faux cough? Try it now! Sure, it might be more complicated, given the fact that they're using fancy cloth napkins, but you can always discreetly slip the napkin into your purse or ideally the trash if you can manage it. This will have the time-tested effect of making food go away from your plate without it having to enter your body for anything more than a few seconds.

Another childhood favorite, discreetly giving your food to the family dog, is not applicable here since there's no dog in sight. Actually, if these people ever had a dog, they probably couldn't resist serving him up in a pomegranate reduction with truffles and haricots verts. Hopefully, they didn't choose tonight to do it. Cough, cough.

Use the Jargon

As you subtly cough up your meal of possibly Fido, you can really help yourself by praising the cuisine using lots of foodie adjectives. For those who consider themselves gastronomes, epicures, locavores, or gourmands, what comes out of your mouth is almost as important as what goes in. Translation: they are wordy so-and-sos. So tell them that the llama bone marrow is "revelatory" and "piquant" and that the octopus has a "complex mouthfeel." You can talk about the "symphony of flavors" that you hear as you "tuck into" the mustardy Brussels sprouts. Say whatever, as long as it sounds really pretentious and you're not coughing up the food at the same time. Bonus points if you can work in the word "artisanal." They love that!

Be Sick or Full

If the above options do not work for you and you are sure you're not going to be able to handle this meal, you need to take drastic measures to save yourself. If you are positive you can't eat any of it, you're going to have to say you're not feeling very well. You can say you and your man went to a local bar and got a bit buzzed before dinner, and now you're feeling queasy. Or you can choose the more clichéd, "I might be coming down with the flu." They might or might not believe you, but they're not going to take the chance of forcing eyeballs down your throat when it might come back up on their nice little table.

If you can manage to eat a little bit of one item, try to. For example, eat some complex and revelatory Brussels sprouts and say, "These are like a party in my mouth." Do what you need to do to have the table cleared and move onto dessert. Carmelized snails in artisanal goat cheese! Yay!

Being Happily Surprised at Your Bridal or Baby Shower

You've just finished doing some invariably messy and unglamorous activity —maybe it's unclogging drains at a dog salon, or Extreme Fever Hallucination Hot Yoga, or a rousing game of paintball—with your best friend, and you're wearing your please-god-don't-let-me-run-into-anyone-I-know sweatpants. Of course this is the day you will be ambushed at your home by the 1,000-kilowatt smiles of twenty of your favorite women (plus thirty other females). They are screaming, "Surprise!" as they raise their glasses of pinkish, fruit-garnished liquid in the air. You are trapped like an antelope surrounded by hungry cheetahs.

Make no mistake—surprise showers are a type of attack. Sure, they might be a *fun attack*, filled with goodwill and love, but they're attacks all the same. I mean, think about it: A large number of people have conspired to enter your home, sneak up on you unawares, and pounce in unison. If that happened under any other circumstances, you'd be pepper spraying the shit out of them.

Shower Psychology

Why, oh why, do women insist on this bizarre ritual? Well, you've had a bit of good luck lately, right? Either you've found the man of your dreams, or you're expecting your first bundle of joy. These ladies love you, and they will be the first to rejoice with you on the big day—some of them might even be forced to wear brown taffeta paisley bridesmaid dresses on your behalf. But first, they're here to make you pay a teeny-weeny price. You're either going to have to play a nonsensical game involving speculation over the size of your stomach, or else undergo the mortification of wearing a penis-shaped hat for three hours. We women are funny that way.

Think of it as hazing into a very elite sorority. These girls are embracing you and welcoming you into the fold—not to mention spending the bulk of a Sunday afternoon with you that they'd rather spend watching *Jersey Shore* reruns. They just want to gently mess with your head while they're at it.

Get Into the Spirit

It's perfectly fine to act thrown off—and embarrassed by your hideously inappropriate attire—for the first ten minutes or so. In fact, it's good to do this—it shows your friends that they did the job right. They got you *good!* Let them savor that depraved pleasure for a little while. After that, though, you're going to have to switch gears from "shock and horror" mode to "I'm just *delighted* to have been trapped here in these terrible sweatpants" mode. Just try to focus on your gratitude for the gesture, rather than your annoyance that it involves a game called "Diaper Piñata." (Oh, how you look forward to seeing that thing explode!)

Look, this isn't rocket science. Just smile and be gracious to everyone, especially the women who worked hard to plan this for you. People will understand if you don't have much time for one-on-one conversation with each of them, but you should at least greet, chat briefly with, and thank each person at the party. Just think, some women couldn't fill a house with other women who loved them—or at least with women who didn't particularly hate them. Not if their *lives* depended on it. So feel the love!

Or, if you absolutely have to, break it down as if it were a paid job. For example, if you have 30 guests who spent $50 each on gifts, and your shower lasts three hours, you're earning a cool $500 an hour, just for smiling and saying thanks. So put on that penis hat and smile.

A Compliment for a Friend's Baby

Well, the big day has come for your close friend or family member—she's given birth to her first baby. Too bad the poor kid looks like a cross between Dwight Eisenhower and a severely misshapen yam.

There's no way around it—you're going to have to compliment this baby. Not just the baby's mere existence or the fact that he/she is a little miracle with ten fully functional fingers and toes, but the baby's superior adorableness. Your friend is waiting for you to say that her offspring is the most eye-pleasing creature you have ever seen, even if she knows better. *Especially* if she knows better.

No matter what you do, you *cannot* tell a woman that her baby is extremely unfortunate looking. Ever. Women don't have babies so that they can be told terrible truths—they have babies so that they can hear lots of coos and "aws," buy little footie pajamas, hear magical music box songs, and picture frolicking lambs in their heads all day. They certainly don't do it so you can say, "That baby's so fugly, I'll bet his incubator had tinted windows."

I mean, think about it: When's the last time anyone ever said, "Here's a picture of our new baby. We welcome your honest feedback"? Right, never. That's because they don't want it. So you're going to have to hold your tongue. When it comes to you and this baby, it is officially Opposites Day. I call this very necessary evil the "crib fib."

Don't Delay!

Ideally, you should start crafting some good crib fibs as soon after birth as possible, not only because your delay would look suspicious, but also because of those freaking adorable skullcaps they slap on babies in the maternity ward. Those hats are the great equalizers of baby heads the world over. They're especially useful when the hat conceals most of the face. (Maybe someday, hospitals will figure this out and start using little ski masks!) But for now, you can say something like, "Aw, she looks *so* cute in her little hat!" That's not 100 percent dishonest, is it? This goes double for those anti-scratch mittens.

A great way to increase your chances of this skullcap scenario is to buy the baby a whole slew of them before he's even born, as a shower gift. Even if your friend hates them and never uses them 364 days of the year, you can almost guarantee she'll throw one on little Igor's head specifically for *your* visit. FYI, this is a secret from the Mom Bag of Tricks and Fakes—having the baby model his or her gifts specifically for the giver. So your friend will be pulling a fake on you, too. Luckily, it will be a fake that happens to cover two of the baby's three eyes.

Like Mother, Like Baby

If you should miss that perfect window when those caps still fit over the child's giant head, never fear (unless the little monster starts gnawing or spitting up on everything you own—then, be very afraid). Try to focus on an attractive feature your friend has and claim that the baby also has it, such as "Look at those big, blue eyes! They're just like momma's!" or "She has your dorsal flipper!" (Yeah, skip that last one.)

Just Be Nice

If all else fails, focus on the fact that this is your friend's child and a sweet, innocent new life. Luckily, you won't need to fake it for too much longer, because most babies get *much* cuter within their first year and grow out of that funky squishing of the head, unless their name is Philip Seymour Hoffman. Aw, imagine him in anti-scratch mittens!

Sadness over Your Friend's Breakup with a Less-Than-Wonderful Guy

Did you know that at the funeral of North Korean autocrat Kim Jong Il, people who didn't cry convincingly enough were sentenced to six months in hard labor camps? Talk about high-stakes faking! You can bet that hundreds of people who would have much preferred to dance around singing, "Ding Dong, the Dictator's Dead," were instead wringing their hands, shrieking in pseudo-agony, and chopping onions on the sly. And so it must be with you, as you react to the news that your friend is finally breaking up with that jerk she's been lugging around.

I mean, this guy is a grade A loser in almost every way. He's selfish, lazy, mean-spirited and the intellectual equal of an amoeba. *And* he has a wandering eye that strays so far someone should round it up and put it in the SPCA. And yet he continues to think he is God's Gift to Women. Let's hope God had the sense to include a gift receipt with this one.

Basically, he's the Kim Jong Il of boyfriends, and he's finally been toppled. How do you pretend not to celebrate with the fervent joy of a thousand repressed societies?

Buy Tubs of Ben & Jerry's and Watch *The Notebook*

Sure, you had your issues with the guy—he was a know-it-all creep who talked down to your friend (when he wasn't busy talking directly at other women's boobs), but for whatever reason, she cared about him, and she's probably grieving the breakup. Your dance of joy would therefore be inappropriate and hurtful, but that doesn't mean you can't derive some enjoyment from the situation. Pop *The Notebook* into the DVD player and start consuming tubs of ice cream like there's no tomorrow, because let's face it, what woman doesn't love shamelessly indulging in swirls of caramel and chunks of brownies while watching Ryan Gosling carry Rachel McAdams up several flights of stairs? We women are unique in that we have our little celebratory rituals for the full range of our emotions, the bad as well as the good. In other words, even our pity parties have awesome food.

And when your friend starts bawling over how much her ex reminds her of Ryan's character (right, because you're *sure* her man also jumped up onto a moving Ferris wheel to ask her out) you can start your own waterworks by lamenting the hours you'll have to spend at the gym to burn off those five pints of Half Baked you just ate. By the end of the movie, she'll be consoling you!

Don't Make Her Defend Him

Another crucial mistake you want to avoid is to force your friend into the position of defending this man. No matter how much of a creep he might have been, she will be compelled to defend him if you attack him. In this way, you're essentially forcing her to recall his finer moments (yes, he took me to Hooters for Valentine's Day, but he paid, and that Lots-A-Tots appetizer was delicious!) and cite his good qualities (he always said he thinks fatties are beautiful!). The next thing you know, she'll be getting all sappy thinking about how "wonderful" he is, and she'll be in danger of a relapse. Nice work.

Focus on Your Friend's Pain

The point is, you don't need to pretend you loved the guy—that's too ambitious, and would seem about as real as Joan Rivers' bone structure. Instead, empathize with your friend's feelings. Think about the losses in your life, how you struggled with them, and how you finally got through them. By drawing from your own experiences, you'll show her that not only have you been there—you survived. And she will, too. If you do this right, it's barely faking at all. And if you've still got the urge to openly celebrate your friend's emancipation from that A-hole, just remember that he might be back next week. And if you don't play nice now, guess who's going to get the Kim Jong Il treatment later?

Having a Great Life at Your High School Reunion

Ah, the old high school reunion—it's an event more full of faking than a bad porno movie. Everyone, it seems, has something to prove—the jocks that they haven't lost 90 percent of their hair and gained twenty pounds, the prom queens that they haven't spent the decade having a zillion kids and gaining twenty pounds, and the nerds that they haven't continued to be ostracized, especially after gaining twenty pounds. Then there are all the nondescript types in between. These folks are just hoping that their extra twenty pounds will make them visible for a change.

Believe it or not, high school isn't an easy time for anyone. Adolescence is a really weird, difficult time, filled with self-doubt, awkwardness, and a fruitless quest for meaning. Adulthood is similar, minus the hickeys.

Hopefully, though, you've reached a more stable place as you stare down your high school reunion. You know yourself better, you've found your niche in the world, and you're at peace with yourself. Notice I didn't say, "You have an eight-figure job, you snagged that neurosurgeon husband, or you live in a gorgeous mansion with your 2.5 kids." (That half-kid is *so* well behaved!) That's because these arbitrary trappings don't say much about who you are, and they're just as random as high school labels. If you go into this event still slapping labels on people, you can bet you'll end up feeling like a loser—again.

Live in the Now

In this case, I recommend a different kind of faking: self-faking. You need to play a little trick on your own brain in order to think about things differently.

Ditch the standard reunion measures of a "good life." Your life doesn't need to be perfect for you to appreciate how much you've changed for the better. Think of the amazing friends you have now, or the fun and challenging job, or the heartbreaks you've overcome (hint—high school is one of them!). No matter where you are on the social or economic ladder, there's no doubt you've grown. Maybe you have an amazing guy who sees you as his prom queen (even after seeing photos of your tragically bad perm and glasses), or maybe you've boldly moved to a cool city far from your hometown. No matter what else, you're a survivor. So when the cliquishness of the old high school hierarchy starts to close in on you, just click your ruby slippers and return to your *real* home—the present. (Note: Real ruby slipper clicking is not recommended. This will make you look totally insane.)

Do It for the Right Reason

What I'm going to say next is going to sound scandalous at first, but here it is: If you're planning to attend your reunion with an "I'll show them!" agenda, you should probably skip it. Yes, I know, I know—that's why literally everyone else is going. To which I will repeat a little piece of wisdom about everyone else deciding to jump off a bridge. (Thanks, Mom).

One of the best ways of proving you've outgrown high school is by outgrowing the high school mentality. If you haven't gotten there yet, maybe what you need is a few more years in the school of life. And that's fine—you can just catch up at the next reunion. In the meantime, you can always fake it for your old classmates on Facebook!

A Phone Conversation While You're Doing Something Else

We live in the age of multitasking—people close business deals while pumping breast milk, poking people on Facebook, and trading their roommates for kayaks on Craigslist.

But did you know that multitasking actually makes you measurably dumber? According to a British study, multitasking causes a ten-point drop in IQ—that's the equivalent of a whole night's lost sleep, and it's twice the drop caused by smoking marijuana! Imagine if you're also smoking marijuana while multitasking! Based on my math, that would add up to—let's see, ten divided by two plus ten is . . . oh, wait, what was I just saying about talking to my spirit animal? Let's just try making Rice Krispie treat pancakes—is there even such a thing? It sounds awesome, and I'm starving!

The point is, when you get on the phone these days, the chances are good that your friends are not sitting next to their old-school wall-anchored telephone, staring straight ahead, their unadulterated focus 100 percent on the words you are speaking. But just in case, here's how to fake your own focus.

Talk to a Mom

One great way to do a zillion things while talking on the phone without a smidgen of guilt is to talk to a mom. No one in the world, no matter what technology they have at their fingertips, could possibly be as distracted as a mom whose kids are present. You can sit there and check your Twitter page while murmuring, "uh-huh," and "okay," and your friend will be permitted approximately six words of adult conversation before she screams, "Jayden! Put that down!" or "Sophia! Share with your brother!" You'll then hear a garbled exchange with the offending child, and she'll return to you with a sigh. "Sorry," she will say.

It's brilliant! You've been watching a YouTube video of a kitten riding on a turtle's back the whole conversation, and *she's* apologizing to you! Well played!

Talk to an Automated Voice Menu

If it's even possible that there's a better phone call to multitask to than a call between you and a frazzled mom, it's the call between you and an automated voice menu. As annoying as automated voice menus can be when you really need help, they are *awesome* to talk to when you just don't care. So just call up and tune out! Check your e-mails or go on Facebook. Do whatever will amuse you while you deal with Ms. Roberta Robot and her warning to, "Please listen carefully, as our menu options have recently changed." Whatever, Roberta, you've been saying that for years now! I know that trick! How 'bout this? "I'll *listen carefully* when *you* listen carefully! Oh what's that? You can't listen carefully, because you're a robot? Well then, it's back to Farmville for me!"

One word of warning: Don't confuse the robot too much, or it will hang up on you. Here's an example:

Roberta: "Please say or indicate which of the following you're calling about. You can say, 'pay bill,' or 'check balance,' or 'hear recent transactions.'"

You: "OMG, Roberta, you are *not* going to believe who they cast in the new *Celebrity Apprentice*! The Incredible Hulk *and* Debbie Gibson? Can't you just picture him turning green while she sings 'Electric Youth'? Brilliant!"

Roberta: "Sorry, I didn't get that."

You: "Yes! Just got a triple-letter score in Scrabble using my Q! Did you even know that 'suq' was a word?"

Roberta: "Your entry was invalid. Please call back at a later time. Goodbye."

Mix and Match

Regarding work or urgent friend calls, my advice is to mix a mental task with a physical task. If you do a menial physical job while talking, you're still leaving a large chunk of your brain open to the conversation. So, to review: a conversation about your friend's horrible husband while doing laundry equals: good; a conversation about your friend's horrible husband while preparing a grueling work presentation and bidding for an antique Chewbacca action figure equals: bad. Likewise, a work conference call while making salad equals: good; a work conference call while e-mailing your BFF about her ovulation-timing difficulties equals: bad.

Where You Are When You're Supposed to Be Home Sick

Remember the time you called in sick with a high fever and flu, and then you ran into your boss at your local bar at 2:00 P.M.? In a flash, you went through the stages of career death: denial, anger, bargaining, and finally, Jack Daniel's. First there was that sickening pit in your stomach as you said hello to her, then there was your sad, awkward attempt at casual conversation, then there was that momentary "aha!" when you thought, "Wait, what's she doing here?" For a millisecond, you thought you'd found a loophole of mutual hooky-playing. Until she explained that she was there for the post-service luncheon for her great aunt's funeral. Ugh.

So, you're not at that job anymore. But like everyone, you still occasionally like to go places when you're supposed to be home sick. Here's how to fake it.

Always Order Jello Shots

This is a piece of advice I never thought I'd have occasion to give, but there it is. I should preface this by saying that if you absolutely need to hit the bar while you're supposed to be home sick, go to an out-of-the-way location. Likewise, if you know where your boss (or whoever you're avoiding) lives, steer clear of that area as well. Taking these simple steps can go a long way toward saving your skin.

But once you are out and about, and you're drinking either way, Jello shots are the way to go. What's that? you might ask. Jello shots? They're the most juvenile, ridiculous frat party drink in the world! Why should I order them?

Hello . . . does no one remember when you were a kid and you had an upset stomach, and Jello was one of the few things you could keep down without puking? Well, if you get caught out on the town when you're supposed to be sick, that Jello could be your saving grace. The only thing better would be chicken soup shots, and they don't exist (I checked). Say, "Well I just wanted a little fresh air, but all my stomach can tolerate is this Jello" (wince stoically). There is *no need* to tell them that your stomach-sparing Jello is spiked with ninety-proof rum. However, if said rum should make you sick enough to vomit during your interaction with your boss, the whole thing could come full circle in a beautiful way.

Be Prepared to Go With It

Let's just imagine that, instead of the job/boss scenario, you faked sickness to get out of a social plan. For example, maybe there's a party on a Saturday night, and you said you were sick on Friday. Then, on Saturday afternoon, whom should you run into at the mall but Ms. Party Host? She smiles and says, "Oh, wow—are you feeling better? Does this mean you'll be able to come tonight?"

Well, I'm sorry to tell you this, but you've managed to get yourself caught in a little trap here. The lure of Saturday afternoon shopping led you to take this wanton risk, and now the steely snare of the trap just clamped down on your leg. In order to save yourself, you may need to gnaw that leg off.

Just put your fake in reverse and say, "I was going to call you later. Yes, I'm feeling much better. What can I bring?" Learn from this experience— you took a gamble, and you lost. Hope that sale at the Gap was worth it!

Go Bare

If you do feel compelled to go to a risky place while you're supposed to be sick, drop your vanity and skip the makeup. Leaving the house without makeup is one of the very best tricks of the fake-sick trade. You know how you diligently apply your makeup each day so you can resemble a halfway normal-looking human? Just do the opposite. The fact is that most women without their makeup look genuinely sick. If you go out sans makeup, your naked face will do most of the lying for you. They'll take one look at you and want to feed you Jello shots!

Your Marital Status or Sexual Preference to Lose the Creep at the Bar

You haven't seen your best girlfriend in almost a month, and the two of you are out at the bar, trying to catch up and have a drink in peace. You're focusing entirely on the conversation—that is truly what this evening is for. You're not tossing your hair, or flashing your cleavage, or leaning over on the bar stools to reveal your thongs and lower back tattoos. So why is that gelled-up, cologne-oozing creep intent on bothering you? He's been ping-ponging back and forth between the two of you with such classy lines as, "Great legs. What time do they open?" and "I seem to have lost my number. Can I borrow yours?" (No, but you can borrow the number to the Bad Breath Hotline. I suggest you call it ASAP.)

For some guys, like this one, there is nothing more irresistible in a woman than total indifference. Fine, but that should be a problem for this dude's shrink, not you and your friend. You need to dispatch this mosquito of a male with a minimum of annoyance. What you have to do is either fake your marital status or your sexual preference. Let's review some of the ways you can do this.

Pretend to Be a Lesbian

One option you can use to get out of this situation is to pretend your sexual preference is for women. However, in our current social climate, I would very strongly urge you to use this approach with extreme caution. The fact is, men absolutely *love* lesbians. In fact, I think men secretly believe that lesbianism is just this awesome thing us girls made up to turn them on even more. Particularly if both parties are attractive, guys don't see lesbianism as shutting them out of the action—quite the opposite. Instead, they just think, "the more, the merrier." And by merrier, I don't necessarily mean gayer.

So if you think that turning to your girlfriend and planting a lingering kiss on her lips is going to make that guy go away, you need to be locked up and given electroshock therapy until you stop thinking that.

If you want to go the lesbian route, you need to go for the "nonlipstick lesbian" approach. Have a picture in your wallet of a woman who looks like your old gym teacher (a recent picture of Al Franken or Bruce Jenner can also double nicely as a butt-kicking lesbian). Birkenstocks and fanny packs are encouraged. Tell the dude your life partner is the extremely jealous type.

Lord of the Ring

The faux ring is the oldest trick in the book, but for a guy like your little barfly, the chance that it's real might be a risk he doesn't want to take. You can get a beautiful, moderately authentic looking Cubic zirconia engagement or wedding ring for between $15 and $24! Just google "fake wedding ring," and you will find plenty of gorgeous options to repel parasites, almost like a flea and tick collar.

If you want to really mess with his head, try a tattoo wedding ring. A tattoo says, in no uncertain terms, *this woman is committed for life— possibly to a Hell's Angel.*

Of course, you don't want to get permanent ink just to chase away some gelled-up freak. That's why you need to get a temporary wedding band tattoo (also available online). Again, emphasize how your tattoo-loving man doesn't take kindly to little weasels hitting on his woman.

Phone a Friend

If you have a good male friend, brother, or other male who owes you something, make a prearranged plan to have him call you or show up at the bar if needed. Just send him a quick text that says "code pretend husband" or some similar signal, and have him show up looking possessive and annoyed.

Note: If you happen to be living in a romantic comedy script, the fake husband is definitely the way to go. Eventually, you will fall in love with him, and you'll all live happily ever after. Except that jerk at the bar—he's on his own.

Not Being Jealous of Your Friend's Recent Success

So, your best friend in the world has landed that coveted promotion, or met the perfect guy, or moved into her dream home (with a pool *and* a hot tub). And you're truly happy for her, really you are. You'd just be a teeny bit happier if you'd also gotten a (slightly better) promotion, or guy, or house, just a smidge before she got hers. *And* if your pool and hot tub also had underwater strobe lights and an awesome, tricked out stereo system.

Envy is a very ugly—but very common—aspect of friendship. We women especially hate feeling it, because our bonds are strong, meaningful, and unrelated to football. So how can you love this woman while simultaneously wishing you could slither into her house and steal her life like some nasty, heartless Grinchette?

I could go on and on about how jealousy stems from insecurity and a lack of fulfillment in our own lives, but instead I will break it down with a simple analogy. After looking at her piece of cake, your piece of cake is looking pretty crappy. The more you focus on her cake, the more you start to feel deprived and resentful. Eating cake with her then becomes more painful than fun, even though she's always been your favorite person to eat cake with. But it's not about her cake; it's about your cake. Wait, why are you eating cake, anyway? I thought you were doing Atkins!

Don't Repress It

The first step to faking happiness when you're secretly jealous is to at least be honest with yourself. Admit to yourself that you are feeling insanely envious, even though you wish you weren't. We women tend to lie to ourselves about jealousy, because it's such an icky emotion to feel. But if you deny your own feelings, they will come out sideways on you. Trust me. Women who repress their jealousy are the same ones who blurt out remarks like, "It's great you could get that promotion—even at your age!" or "He's a real keeper—it's so awesome that he's open-minded about weight," or "I thought hot tubs were just for swingers." Don't be that girl—you'll end up with no friends to be jealous of.

Lie, Lie, Lie!

Okay, so once you've been honest with yourself about your jealousy, the next step is to be completely and utterly dishonest with your friend about it. You absolutely *cannot* tell her about this feeling, or sulk about it, or project anything other than total support and joy for her. You will need to make your best effort to make sure your voice does not convey tones of bitterness, sadness, or annoyance. At the same time, you don't want to sound like a sugarcoated, five-exclamation-points phony, because she will see right through that. No one said this task would be easy—it's like delivering an Academy Award–winning performance without the pay or red carpet swag. The fact is, if you're close, your friend probably already knows that this is killing you. And she will appreciate your summoning up your support and love even more.

Take Inventory

So you've faced your yucky feeling and you've lied until your pants literally caught on fire. Congratulations! After you've extinguished your fiery, ashen pants, the next step is to figure out why your friend's good fortune hurt so much. This means taking a long, hard look at your own life, and figuring out what's missing. Do you need a career change? Is your love life somehow lacking in spark? Is your desire for a hot tub rooted in a misguided longing for time travel? You need to answer these questions for yourself and then make life changes accordingly. Do whatever it takes so you won't be blind-sided by jealousy again. Then politely thank the Academy, your mom, and sweet baby Jesus for the friendship Oscar you've won (for Best Supporting, naturally!). Then stroll down your imaginary red carpet in your crumbling ember soot pants. Oh look, now you've made Lady Gaga jealous!

Being Happy When You've Had a Horrible Day

Wow, have you ever had a lousy day—you got chewed out by your boss for something that totally wasn't your fault, you got in a stupid argument with your husband about his habit of forgetting to flush the toilet, and your pet goldfish all dropped dead from some bizarre goldfish disease (you discovered this because your husband forgot to flush the toilet). On top of all this, you have PMS that makes you feel as vulnerable as the boy in the plastic bubble, and—oh yeah—it's Monday. All you want to do is burrow under your covers and cry yourself to sleep. In a perfect world, you could do just that, but in a perfect world there would probably be no such thing as crying in the first place and goldfish would never die.

There are plenty of reasons you might need to fake being happy. Maybe you're going out with friends whose problems make yours look like a unicorn ride in a field filled with four-leaf clovers. Maybe you promised to take your kid to the mall to meet Santa Claus. Or maybe you have to go on one of those grueling client dinners where you must turn on a phony perma-smile. Whatever the reason, you need to fake okay-ness for just a little while. Do it in memory of your poor goldfish—you know that Bella, Edward, and Jacob would want you to be happy.

Go to a Sad Movie

If you have any say at all in what to do with your evening, I suggest steering things toward a movie. Movies are excellent—they're semi-social yet mostly private, they provide the cover of darkness, and they present the opportunity for emotional catharsis. I would further suggest that you arrange to see a heartbreakingly sad movie. This way, you can sit there in the dark with your friends or family and cry your eyes out openly. You can pretend to be reacting to the movie while enjoying a private pity party over all that went so terribly wrong with your day. Then, after the movie is over, you will be purged of every last bit of sadness, having indulged it for two hours straight. You will also be able to sleep like a baby when you get home, since crying totally wears you out. That movie should win an Oscar!

Have a Drink Cutoff

Indulging in a limited amount of alcohol may relax and calm you, and remind your sad little brain cells that tomorrow is, in fact, another day. However—and I can't stress this enough—if you cross that invisible line, you can go quickly from peacefully buzzed fun girl to disastrously drunken sob story. Nothing is worse for your career, friendships, or family than for you to be crying into an Appletini while lamenting, "Nobody understands how hard it is to be me." I know, I know, it's a coping mechanism—but it can easily turn on you. Set a two-drink maximum—one for professional outings.

Focus on Humor

Stephen King once said, "Humor is almost always anger with its makeup on." Anger with makeup on—yep, it's either humor or Courtney Love.

But King has a point. Humor is an awesome way to take aim at life's heartbreaks in a fun and empowering way. In fact, it's often used in anger management classes. So when you think about this lousy day you've had, what's the next emotion that pops up after sadness? That's right—anger.

It was totally unfair of your boss to blame you for the rampant interoffice paper clip theft! It was just plain mean for your goldfish to die in less than a month, and it was inconsiderate of your husband to do such an incomplete job on their watery funerals. You're mad! So channel that anger into wit—make fun of your husband, tell a hilarious anecdote about your boss, mock the way your goldfish's poop never quite broke off from their butts. People prefer anger-turned-to-wit much more than sadness turned to soggy tears. And by the next day, maybe even you'll be able to laugh.

Good Table Manners When You're Invited to a Family Dinner

Did you know that in addition to his other not-so-sterling qualities, Adolf Hitler had hideous table manners? Yep, according to notes taken by a rather catty high-ranking Nazi, the Führer bit his fingernails (!) and played with his icky mustache during meals. He also "gorged on cake," was a "mechanical" chewer, and suffered from flatulence.

Now, you certainly know better than to leave fingernail bits on the dinner table, but your table manners do leave something to be desired. And that something is a giant bib.

Not only are you a natural klutz with food and silverware, you haven't a clue about the weird encoded rules of table manners. It seems grossly unfair to you, how easily you can accidentally be offensive without meaning one bit of harm. Seriously, your elbows are just comfortable there!

So you've been invited to a large, extended family dinner celebrating a milestone birthday for your Great Aunt Millie. Hopefully, your family knows that you are not an infamous horrible dictator and perpetrator of mass genocide, but they sure don't trust you with a salad fork. Time to put on your faking cap and get to work.

Wait!

According to the Modern Manners Guy, Adam Lowe, from *www.quick anddirtytips.com*, patience is a very important virtue of table manners. This especially applies to being considerate of your fellow diners. For example, you should wait to sit down until you've helped those who need help being seated. You should wait to take bread from a breadbasket until you've offered some to others. You should wait to begin eating until the host or hostess has started to eat. Oh, and you should wait until you've finished chewing to answer a question someone has asked you. If answering means treating the whole table to an insider's view of your partially masticated mushroom ravioli, postponing your reply is not considered rude. However, if someone is choking on a chicken bone and you know the Heimlich, waiting would be sort of terrible.

About Elbows

If you're a bit of a table manners novice, you might wonder, "What is so horrible about elbows?" They are just innocuous joints, maybe a little on the pointy side but not offensive in any way. It's not like people are outside sticking their elbows into the dirt or spreading elbow STDs (I hope)! So why is there this bizarre rule about no elbows on the table? One theory, according to Helena Echlin at *www.chow.com*, is that if your elbows are on the table, you're probably hunched over your food in a way that makes you look like a crazed Neanderthal. In order to avoid this hunched-over posture, imagine what would happen if the table were suddenly whisked out from under you. Would you fall? That means you're hugging that table a little bit too hard. If you love that food, set it free. If it comes back to you, you definitely ate too much.

Forks, Spoons, Knives, and Napkins

Okay, now on to the tricky part—silverware and napkins. You've been using this stuff since you were a kid, but there's a difference between pretending your spoon is a choo-choo train and properly using silverware for its designated purpose. And for whatever reason, fancy-schmancy dinner party types like to set up sadistic tests for the rest of us by having a zillion different identical-looking implements lined up together like multiple choice questions. Trying to choose the right one is like MacGyver trying to choose the right wire to snip, one of which disarms the bomb; the other— blows the effing place sky high.

It's a snobby little test, to be sure, but there's an excellent cheat sheet. Modern Manners Guy, Lowe, says silverware usually goes from the outside in. So the first fork on the outside should be used for the salad, the first spoon for the soup, etc. Of course, if there's something truly bizarre on the outside of your lineup, like a melon baller or plastic beach shovel, don't start with those. *Everyone* knows plastic beach shovels are for dessert!

A Friendship When You Can't Stand the Girl

Okay, I can just picture all you sanctimonious, high-and-mighty types wagging your fingers and saying, "Why would you ever need to fake a friendship when you can't stand someone? That's like lying, and lying is *wrong . . .*"

First of all, I commend you for your moral excellence, and for the fact that you've managed to live this long without ever venturing out of your house. Kudos! Not many people can say that they've gained all of their life experience from reruns of *Diff'rent Strokes,* but you are clearly a special case. I wish you nothing but rainbows and tumbling puppies in your magical world. Seriously!

For those of you who leave your homes for hours at a time, a sad reality has probably occurred to you. Sometimes, you may feel compelled to fake even the sacred bonds of friendship. Maybe your abrasive boss has taken a shine to you and wants to be your BFF. Maybe there's an endearingly nerdy, awkward friend-of-a-friend who worships the ground you walk on. Or maybe your mom has this terrible idea that since you're an adult now, the two of you should be "girlfriends." The list goes on and on.

The reality is, most fake friendships are temporary. Either they grow on you and graduate to real friendship, or they fade mercifully away. Until then, there's no need to crush this person's spirit. Think of all your mom has done for you!

Fake It on Facebook

If ever there was a place meant for fake friendship to grow and flourish while barely touching the real world, it is Facebook. Social networking is an ideal place to carry out "friendships" that you don't necessarily need to become friendships. Make sure your faux girlfriend is your Facebook friend, and try to give her as much virtual love and attention as you can manage. Give thumbs up to any of her statuses that you can remotely stand or any pictures of universally great things, like kittens or chocolate cake. Try your best to keep this friendship as confined to the virtual realm as you can. In this way, you can be sitting at your computer thinking, "I can't stand you, you crazy bleep!" while typing something more like "Yay! You go, girl!" Maintaining this contradiction is much easier in the virtual world than in real life, so do your best to keep it unreal. If your "friend" tries to extend this connection into real life, you should either try to politely decline invitations to get together, or else make those real-world hangouts memorably bad. Show up with a disgusting cold, maybe, or whine about your PMS the entire time. After a few of these, she will begin to think, Facebook friendship equals: good, real life friendship equals: horrible and potentially germ spreading.

Keep It at the Office

Ah, work friendships. With the right person, they can be a saving grace for those hours spent within the cubicle walls. With the wrong person, they feel like a second full-time job. Yet there are circumstances, usually dictated by subtle and horrible office politics, in which you must "make nice" with someone who couldn't make nice if someone handed her the recipe. This is unfortunate, but the point is this: eight hours is a long time.

And really, those eight hours should be more than enough time to have to contribute to a faux friendship. Try to limit your after-work interactions with your faux friend to workplace group activities, such as happy hours or book clubs. These activities will still fall under the heading of "workplace" and will be buffered by other coworkers. You should *not* have to go with your boss to get bikini waxes or to a Justin Bieber concert with her and her tween daughter. So feel free to politely decline invitations that feel too personal and just plain weird. If necessary, use your significant other as an excuse. If you don't have a significant other, I'm not necessarily saying you should go out and get one just to keep this lady at bay, but . . . you know, if you wanted to, I'm not going to stop you.

Disdain for the Trashy Reality TV Show Your Friends All Hate (but You Secretly Love)

Here is a rough transcript of a recent conversation between you and your friends. (Sorry I've been secretly recording your conversations. Please don't sue.)

Friend 1: "OMG, have you seen that show about the former '80s child stars who all live together on that boat and are dared to eat each other's disgustingly cooked meals in order to win the heart of the eligible dolphin fisherman bachelor? I think it's called *Celebrity Bachelorette Bad Chef: High Seas Challenge* or something."

Friend 2: "That show is *so* stupid, so demeaning to women, and the food!? Repulsive. And who wants to marry a dolphin fisherman, anyway? Dolphins are the smartest animals around. That guy's an idiot."

You: "Yeah, it's um . . . really bad . . . That's . . . a bad show, all right."

Friend 1 and Friend 2, in horrified unison: "Oh my god, you like it!" (pointing, laughing) "She likes it!"

[You cry. End of scene]

This scene could have been prevented. Yes, you *are* secretly intrigued by the crazy antics—and very questionable seaweed and jellyfish recipes—of those former '80s celebrity bachelorettes at sea. And you *do* happen to think that dolphin fisherman Eric *is* kind of dreamy (and let's face it—dolphins are creepy, always smirking and making those clicking sounds). But the truth is, some reality shows just aren't cool to like. And why should you be the one getting pointed and laughed at?

Know the Jargon

If you want to sound convincing about not liking that reality show, or any other reality show you might secretly love, you have to talk the talk. You don't want to critique it on its entertainment value (because we all know reality shows are ridiculously entertaining), but rather on its impact on society. You see, everyone gets their feathers ruffled about the use of the word "reality" to describe these shows, taking this as a sign that our "real" world is bound for hell in the proverbial handbasket. It's so silly, because *everyone* knows these shows contain as much actual reality as Heidi Montag's boobs. They're like the modern equivalent of soap operas, except with fewer comas. So this maneuver will be a double fake: You have to fake not liking something that is, itself, a fake. Say things like, "It's such a pathetic commentary on our society that . . ." and trail off and shake your head disapprovingly. Someone will pick up that thread for you, I guarantee. Another popular refrain among reality show haters is that the stars are "famous for being famous." You can always sarcastically say, "I love it that you don't actually have to *do* anything or have any *talent* to become a star." Of course, some reality stars might argue that eating rat testicles while riding a unicycle is, indeed, doing something.

Like the Show "Ironically"

One coping mechanism that is very popular among conflicted, closeted reality TV show fans is the liberal use of "irony." As in, fake irony. It's very common to hide behind irony when liking things that are terribly embarrassing to like. So rather than displaying flat out sincerity, which is the equivalent of showing up at work naked, we cloak our love in eye rolling, protective-irony wear. Say, "Yeah, *Celebrity Bachelorette Bad Chef: High Seas Challenge* is my guilty pleasure." By saying "guilty pleasure," you're acknowledging that you know the show is stupid and you don't really like it-like it, you just watch it because it's kind of cool to like things you don't like. Everyone will nod vigorously, and some might say, "Me, too!"

Next, follow up with a mocking commentary of the cast, something like, "Did you see that episode where dolphin fisherman Eric says he's looking for his soulmate to eat dolphin burgers with forever? Total *freak*!" Never mind that when you watched it, you solemnly mouthed to the TV, "I'll eat dolphin burgers with you, Eric," and touched his face on the screen. It's like when you secretly loved that nerdy boy in seventh grade but disowned him in front of the cool girls. Be prepared for a bit of irony-sickness.

Distress When You Get Pulled Over for Speeding or Running a Red Light

It's just one of those days: You're running late for work, and your cell phone is dead so you can't even call your boss. You're slurping coffee while feverishly racing down some back roads shortcut. Right at the stroke of 9:00 A.M., when things could not seem to get any worse, you see flashing blue lights in your rear view, and you know you're nowhere near a Kmart sale. Yep, things just got worse—you're getting pulled over.

The stony-faced cop waits for a semi-eternity before stepping out of his vehicle. You're cursing to yourself as this guy approaches you and says, "License and registration please, ma'am."

Yes, things got even worse still—someone has called you *ma'am*.

In movies, people who get pulled over always advise each other to "stay cool," but that is stupid advice. Police officers do not want you to stay cool—just the opposite. They want to see that they have an impact, that they have power, and that they are more than just the former football champ who briefly got a little fat before discovering that it's cool to play with guns. You need to let him see how powerful he is without being overtly manipulative. Boy, oh boy, I hope you did your hair and makeup today.

"No, Officer"

Listen carefully, because here's how it's going to go. This unsmiling young man is going to look over your documents skeptically, then look at you, and say, "Do you know how fast you were driving today, ma'am?" or "Do you know, ma'am, why, ma'am, I pulled you over today, ma'am?"

Most likely you know exactly why he pulled you over and approximately how fast you were driving. But under no circumstances should you give a know-it-all response. When an officer asks you this, he is doing it so he can tell you. It's a big deal for them—sort of like their Big Reveal. They want to inform you of your reckless speed, so that you can be shocked by what you've learned. Basically, they want to blow your mind—so let it be blown! Say, "Oh my goodness. I had *no idea* I was going that fast!"

This will be hugely gratifying to the ego of a police officer, and the ego is the ticket-issuing center of the cop brain.

About Crying

Many women have sworn by crying as a means of getting out of a ticket. I am here to tell you a big, horrible secret—cops are onto this game. It's been in movies, it's been in TV shows, and it has infiltrated pop culture. Unless your cop is also a monk, he's heard about this trick. What you need to think about before you decide to start sobbing hysterically is: how gorgeous are you, honestly? Because, in order for the full-fledged cry to be effective, you are going to have to be at least an eight, if not a ten on the hotness scale. If you are a mere mortal cutie, Officer Stoneheart might originally react but then have the backlash feeling that you're playing him for a fool. This will cause him to give you a bigger ticket than he originally intended.

Don't worry, though. Tears still have their place. My recommendation is the "cry with dignity" option. With this, you set your face stoically, answer his questions politely, and let a single tear stream down your face. Let him see how you're fighting to maintain your composure, but you just couldn't stop that one tear. This approach, if you're even moderately attractive, will be emotionally devastating to the cop psychology. Here is a woman who tried *not* to break down, but who showed feminine vulnerability through one beautiful tear. You're not immune to his power to crush you, but you would never try to play him with overacted waterworks. What a lady.

How do you get this stoic tear? I recommend carrying some eye drops (not Visine—that's for potheads) and quickly administering them while pretending to look for your documents. If not, think of the death of your first pet.

Knowing Someone to Get a Dinner Reservation

There's a hot new restaurant in town, and this place is as exclusive as one of those dorky-sounding secret societies that George Bush belonged to at Yale. I mean, this place rejects more people than the judges of American Idol, and everyone loves a place that rejects them. Why, oh why, do human beings automatically crave the acceptance of those who spurn us? It's so masochistic and pointless, so self-esteem crushing. What drives this bizarre human obsession?

I don't know. To find the answer to this big question, I would suggest seeking out the works of the great philosophers, reading up on psychology, or re-watching the "Soup Nazi" episode of Seinfeld.

Anyway, the fact exists: This restaurant is super-snobby, and you and your friends have even started an unofficial competition to see who will be the first to score a reservation. You're dying to be able to casually tell your pals, "Oh, hey, I got a reservation at ___" and watch as they savagely rip each other to shreds to be your Plus One for the evening. This priceless scene cannot be acquired simply through your good looks and personality; once again, you're going to have to fake it.

Know the Reservationist

One person who has a great deal of power to make or break your restaurant dream is the reservationist. This is a harried, multitasking individual who is telephonically manipulated and abused all day. Yet this individual also has the ability to squeeze people in as needed. It doesn't sound as cool as knowing the chef, but it's more likely to actually work. Here's why.

Sadly, the whole "I know the chef" or "I know the owner" thing has gotten a bit played out—restaurants have become savvy to this game. In fact, it's generally assumed that if you really are a friend of the chef, you'd just call your pal directly, and he or she would get you on the list.

If you pretend to know the reservationist, though, you *are* calling your "friend" directly. It's still a risky venture, but it's less expected than the "chef" routine. The reservationist is used to being treated like someone to brush past, an insignificant peon. She'll probably be surprised to be called by name and addressed personally. Plus, it takes supersized cojones to call and say, "I know you," when you don't.

Name Game

If you are determined to pretend to know the owner or chef of a restaurant, it's crucial that you do your basic homework on the person you're pretending to know. For example, according to Kim Severson of the *San Francisco Chronicle*, reservation seekers to the popular Café Kati frequently call and claim to know "Kati." Well, they may as well claim to know Santa Claus, because "Kati" doesn't exist—the name is a combination of the two owners' names. This is just sloppy work, my friends! If you are really that eager to get into this restaurant, you should be willing to do at least some basic online research. If you aren't sure about the details, don't elaborate!

Become a Food Blogger

This is possibly your best bet for getting into your coveted dining spot. Yes, I know, there are probably more food bloggers in existence today than dust mites, but you're going to do it right.

To start with, you're going to show up in person to make your reservation. This often gives a prospective diner a leg up anyway, since the phone lines are likely as tied up as a radio station having a call-in contest.

The next step is to get some press credentials. There are several organizations online that allow bloggers to acquire press credentials for a fee. Some of these even have official-looking photo IDs for extra authenticity. Then put on some professional, polished-looking clothes, and show up there with your press credentials, saying you'd like to write a review of the restaurant. Keep your cool if they say yes—no gushing. Save it for the review you'll put up on your faux blog, just before you shut the operation down and accept the prize money from your friends.

Having a Birthday to Get a Free Dessert at a Restaurant

You've worked exceptionally hard this week, juggling five different projects at work, cleaning your house from top to bottom, and increasing your cardio and lifting workouts to the point that your muscles feel like broken rubber bands. On top of this, you've had a lousy cold all week. Only recently have you started to get your taste buds back, and what your taste buds want is dessert.

You have plans to go out with some friends on Friday, and you feel as though you deserve a little treat. But you are a little short on funds, and you don't feel like springing for dessert. Frankly, you don't feel you should have to. It's not literally your birthday, but you feel like it should be. You want to celebrate yourself. It's a week that demands cake, and like Marie Antoinette, you want to "let them (and you)" eat it—for free. But unlike Marie, you don't want to be busted and metaphorically beheaded for acting like a schmuck.

Time to fake it like a pro. As Lennon and McCartney said, "You say it's your birthday—it's my birthday too." No, seriously. I'm going to pretend it's my birthday too. Let's just not go to the same place, okay?

Say It's Your "Born Again" Birthday

One way to possibly confuse and embarrass the restaurant staff into giving you free cake is to say that as of today, you've been *born again*. Note the alarmed, deer-in-headlights look on the waiter or maître d's face as they try to figure out how to handle this controversial request from this possibly insane person. Tell them that, since you just today found Jesus

Christ and accepted him into your heart as your personal savior, it qualifies as a second birthday for you. Be sure your friends, who you can claim are your sponsors in AA, nod solemnly and say, "Amen," or "Praise Him," when you say this. Tell them how important it is to you, after your years living in darkness as an alcoholic and drug addict, that you celebrate this beginning of your new life.

If you have the guts to actually try this one—and can keep a straight face—I expect it might work. The staff would probably rather give you the cake and get you out of there than cause a scene. Imagine if you called the newspapers the next day and said, "Blah Blah Restaurant would not give me cake for my Born Again Birthday!" They will want no part of that. Note: If you claim to be a recovering alcoholic, maybe don't order booze. Or, conversely, have a relapse and order lots of booze. As long as you pay for that, it'll all be cool.

Get a Fake ID

Many of us have gone to the trouble to get fake IDs, usually when we were teenagers for drinking purposes. You just go to some friend-of-a-friend's shady garage workshop, where they give you a passable picture and a name like "Iris Dunderhoff." Then you go out and attempt to buy drinks with it—sometimes it works; often it doesn't. Bartenders and liquor store proprietors are exceedingly alert to fake IDs from minors. But underpaid waitresses at the Olive Garden can't see them coming from a mile away—especially if you're using yours to get cake.

You might have to plan this maneuver just a little bit ahead of time. There are quite a few resources online for getting fake IDs—not that I am promoting these in any way, shape or form. For smaller, nonchain restaurants, you probably won't even need formal proof for a one-time cake fake. Give it a try without the ID first.

If you do need ID, I advise choosing an embarrassing, undesirable birthday, such as 40. I would have to say that the percentage of people who get fake IDs to falsely claim that they are forty is about negative 25 percent. No one will look at your fake-forty ID and automatically think "cake scam." I mean, how pathetic is that?? If you get the cake, not pathetic at all!

Having Read the Book at a Book Club Meeting

It was a month ago you were "assigned" the book to read for your book club (the title involves some combination of bees, wives, and daughters), and boy, has it been a short month. The club meets tonight, and you haven't cracked that thing open at all.

Maybe it's something about the idea of being forced to read an assigned book when you're not in college anymore, or maybe you are sick of reading about bees, or maybe you've begun to notice that your book club is really just an excuse to drink copious amounts of wine and gossip about your boss's recent stomach stapling surgery. But the fact remains, you are a book club delinquent. You hardly ever start these books, much less finish them, and so far no one is the wiser. But sooner or later, someone's going to say something about your lack of insightful comments. And one of these days, your boss's stomach stapling will become less intriguing. (Although OMG, I heard now that she can't eat, she's become a total alcoholic!)

You don't want to get kicked out of this club, though, so you're going to have to play along a little bit. This means doing some lazy research on *The Beekeeper's Stepdaughter's Bittersweet Honey Society*, stat.

Read Synopsis, First and Last Chapters

A great way to get an initial feel for the tone, writing, and the plot of a book is to read an online synopsis, then the first couple of chapters and the last one. Book synopses are easier than ever to find—just consult Wikipedia. Read as much of it as you can manage—you can do that, can't you?

I would also suggest you read the first few chapters, as well as the last. This is just so that you can get a sense of the author's style and tone. You can use this to either praise or complain about the style at your club. You can say, "Oh, I thought the author's prose style was really wordy," or "I don't think telling the story from the point of view of a pigeon was a very effective device."

You may also be lucky enough to be able to use the trump card of book critiques—hating the ending. This is very popular in book clubs. Just flip to the last chapter, and if it seems to you that maybe the ending is a bit unresolved, or worse, flat out sad, you've just hit the book club lottery. Make sure you are the first one to say, "Am I the only one who hated the ending of this book?" and your friends will chime in with, "Oh my God!! You are *so* right!" If you are the first person to mention hating the ending, you really don't have to say anything else. You've earned the right to sit back, drink your wine, and wonder who else hasn't read the book.

Discuss the Likeability of Characters

At every single book club I have ever attended, the conversation eventually works its way around to the likeability of the book's characters. This is due to the deep-seated tendency of the female psyche to engage in gossip. Even as we are discussing a literary work, we tend to fall into the catty habit of dissecting characters based on who we *like* or *don't like*. It's really the same as workplace gossip about people we know, except it's guilt-free. So it's pretty much always safe to say something like, "Am I the only one who thought Jane Eyre was a little bit of a bitch? It's like she thought she was so special and classy." Best of all, you really can't get this stuff "wrong," because it's an opinion. So you transition smoothly between insulting your immediate supervisor at work (her skirts are made for tweens!) and insulting Hilly Holbrook from *The Help* (she *so* deserved to eat that nasty chocolate pie!). It's all just another girly bitchfest! Yay!

Having Met a Celebrity to Be Relevant to a Conversation

You're hanging out at a party with some ultra cool, status-conscious people you want to impress, and they are dropping more names than you're dropping hors d'oeuvres. Not only do you feel like a big nobody for not having met any celebrities, you are getting some weird looks for your klutzy inability to hold onto your pigs-in-blankets. Why are you taking so many hors d'oeuvres, anyway? Nervous eating is not the answer!

You feel like if you don't come up with an interesting celebrity story in the next few minutes, you are going to be pushed to the periphery of this conversation and be completely forgotten. It's to the point where you're halfway tempted to officially name this next cheese canapé Ryan Gosling before you drop it, so you can drop a "name." Yep, naming the appetizers, that'll get you somewhere—most likely out the door, escorted by security.

Faking a celebrity encounter is not all that difficult, really—as long as you don't overdo it. The key is to be subtle, vague, and not too greedy. Speaking of greedy, enough with the mini quiche, already!

Take a Celebrity Phone Call!

Maybe you're feeling shy, and you don't think you have the confidence to tell a good celebrity story. Don't worry—just fake a celebrity phone call!

Yep, for a fee, you can arrange to have a fake (or real!) call from a celebrity made to your phone. There are various services out there that offer fake calls, complete with caller ID, from Barack Obama, Angelina Jolie, Beyonce, or Brittney Spears. Imagine having your phone ring and caller ID says, "Brad Pitt," but you just decide to let it go to voice mail? How cool are you?

Other services actually allow for prerecorded or customized voice mails from celebrities like Hilary Duff, Manny Ramirez, or ICE T. For a price, you can get the celebrity to leave a voice message reciting a script you've specified, calling you by name. They can leave you a birthday message, wish you a happy Valentine's Day (take that, ex-boyfriend) or just say, "Hi!" All you have to do is say, "Wow, I just got a call from ICE T, want to hear the message?" Then hit play, turn on speaker, and watch their amazement.

For a higher price, you can get certain celebrities to actually make a live phone call to you. This shows some serious commitment to the idea of knowing a celebrity. The most famous person I was able to find for this service was Lou Ferrigno, a.k.a., The Incredible Hulk. Still, though, what an unforgettable party trick—if you're friends with The Hulk, no one will want to get on your bad side!

Keep It Ordinary

When concocting a story about a celebrity sighting or meeting, be sure to avoid the type of material that sounds lifted straight from TMZ. As tempting as some exciting whopper would be, you have to resist and focus on the everyday details. For example, rather than saying, "I saw Sean Penn lynching a paparazzi from a volleyball net," you should say, "I saw Sean Penn eating a chili dog while walking with his son in LA." (Note: Make sure Penn has a son, is not a vegetarian, and that you've been to LA.) If you need ideas for the kinds of everyday stuff that's best for fakery, I would advise consulting *US Weekly's* photo feature called "Just Like Us." Of course, they're not remotely like us, but this photo display makes it seem that way by capturing them in super ordinary or banal moments (grocery shopping, wedgie picking). Keep in mind, though, that this is just a guide—you can't describe the exact image shown in the picture, in case someone sees it. For example, *US Weekly* has a pic of Russell Crowe picking a booger (ick). To be on the safe side, you need to switch *both* the celeb and the embarrassing act. Switch the star to Mickey Rourke, and have him hocking a loogie or brushing dandruff out of his abundant hair. Perfect!

Knowing Someone's Name Who You Don't Remember Meeting

You're at a work convention, or a social event, or just walking down the street minding your own business, and a person you don't for the life of you remember meeting screams, "Tanya! Oh my god! It's so great to see you again, Tanya!" (By the way, your name *is* Tanya, right? If not, can I just call you that from here on out? It's just easier for me to remember.)

Anyway, this woman cannot stop repeating your name, which she has absolutely *nailed* despite the fact that you could not recall hers if a gun were pointed directly at the head of your firstborn. It's as if she's super-proud of her memory skills, which, given the fact that you don't even remember the fact that she has ever existed, are freakishly impressive.

This is bad. You've tried little memory tricks, name recall exercises (i.e., Nancy dresses fancy), but nothing works. Unless someone has left a major and lasting impression on you, you tend to draw a massive blank. Oh, Tanya. That's just so *you*.

This is a common conundrum in social interactions. Particularly in the business world, where people hobnob all day long, it's hard to retain all of these names. Most people are visual learners, so it's easier to remember a face than a name. It's a shame people can't just greet each other the way dogs do, through mutual butt-sniffing. Sadly, business professionals frown on that.

Don't Try to Guess

Trying to guess a person's name might be tempting, but it can also make you look even more ridiculous than you did at the outset. I would say you should only do it if you're relatively sure you're close. The fact is, sometimes the pieces of information we swear are retained knowledge are really weird little judgey bits of our unconscious. For example, if you think that sales rep's name is "Dick," and it turns out to be "Rick," fine. You were close enough that guessing was not so bad. But if you think his name is "Dick" and his name is "Xavier," then that might be more about your unconscious editorializing your first impression of him. Guessing "Dick" in that circumstance would probably turn out to be unfavorable for you. So if you swear that name is on the tip of your tongue, you can venture a guess, but make sure you're pulling it from your memory, not your opinion.

Compliment Their Memory

According to Gretchen Rubin at *www.happiness-project.com*, you can defuse your poor memory by praising the other person's excellent memory. This might mean some over-the-top gushing, but it might be necessary. You can say, "Wow, I'm really impressed that you remember my name—it's been a while!" By focusing on the excellence of their memory skills, you're softening any potential insult implied by not remembering their name. You can even joke that you're going to remember them as "Person with the Awesome Memory." Actually, no, just learn their real name—you don't have the extra storage space for lengthy joke names.

Introduce Them to Someone Else

Another fine trick recommended by Rubin is to introduce your new pal to a third party in your midst. Beckon over a friend or business associate, and say to the unknown person, "I'd like to introduce you to Joe Smith." At this point, custom dictates that the mystery person will state his/her name and shake Joe Smith's hand. If possible, you might want to have a go-to "memory buddy" who you can turn to for this one-sided introduction when you need it. In return, you can step in for them and be the third party introduction assistant when they need it.

If all else fails, there's nothing like searing humiliation to prod your memory the next time you see the person. When you meet him/her again, his/her face will induce a panic-filled recall of "that person who made me look like a complete idiot in front of a bunch of people." So don't you worry, Mom—I'll never forget you again.

Being Hard of Hearing to Avoid Talking to a Blabbermouth Cab Driver

Wow, this business trip—to a suburb of Detroit in January—has taken a lot out of you. For the past seventy-two hours, you've been shaking hands, trading business cards, and smiling like it's going out of style. In fact, for you smiling *has* gone out of style. It is *so* three days ago.

Your flight, which was delayed in the first place, has landed, and you've waited at the baggage carousel for a small eternity with the same sneezing, shoe-removing passengers you endured on the plane. Finally, you've retrieved your bags, have gotten into a cab and are headed home. All you want to do is sit in the car and space out until you can go home and space out in front of the TV.

Oh, but your cab driver isn't having that. He's got a full cup of Star-bucks in his console, approximately sixty-five years of wisdom to share with you, and twenty minutes for a long, leisurely drive.

"So, where are you coming from?" he asks, his voice full of eager delight, as though he hasn't talked to anyone in a while. And possibly, he hasn't. Now, he's thinking this is going to be like an episode of *Taxicab Confessions*. You're thinking it's going to be more like an episode of *CSI* if he doesn't clam up.

My Ears Are Popping!

If you've just come off a plane, then you can easily pretend not to hear what this man is yammering about by claiming that your "ears are pop-ping." By the way, the medical term for this pressure in the ears is "baro-trauma," if you want to sound more credible (although you shouldn't exactly need a doctor's note to shut this dude up!). Explain that you think you might have done some damage to your eardrums. If he persists in trying to talk, respond with "Sorry?" then progress to ruder, increasingly loud responses such as, "What?" or finally "Huh?" until he becomes totally annoyed. After a while, he'll either turn on the radio or start jabbering on that walkie-talkie of his.

Use Sign Language

This one is rather extreme, and should be deployed only in the direst situations. To convince him that you are hard of hearing, you can answer his questions in American Sign Language. Don't know sign language? Me neither! Just fake it. Use signs that seem roughly as though they mean things, and do it rapidly so he won't be able to tell they're not real. (Note: If, like me, you only know one legitimate ASL sign, and that is "I love you," *do not sign this to the cab driver.* This could take your evening in a whole other, undesirable direction.) Of course, by trying to talk in sign language, you are taking a calculated risk—he might have a deaf loved one and be 100 percent fluent. In that case, he either is going to find you extremely offensive (which might be good, except he's driving you and your life is in his hands), or he'll try to rapid-fire sign back to you (not good, for the same exact reason). If he actually takes his hands off the wheel and you scream, "Stop!" I suppose your little ruse will be up. Well played, cab driver, well played.

Long Phone Call

Probably the best approach to avoiding the painfully energetic conversation of a chatty cab driver is the use of electronic devices. I personally favor making or taking a phone call that will last the entire trip. But I thought the whole idea was to avoid conversation, you might protest. Well, kind of. The whole idea is to avoid mind-numbing, mile-a-minute cab driver conversations about sciatica pain or his granddaughter's goth-themed orthodontia. Call your best friend, your husband—even your mom, if necessary, and have a low-maintenance conversation about TV shows, news stories, how your dogs or kids acted while you were gone, anything! Establish a code, such as "cab-blabber" to let them know you'll need them for the duration. If you feel guilty, just give the guy an extra tip. A tip is worth a thousand words!

Politeness When You Bump Into Someone You've Been Avoiding

You should have known better than to allow yourself to be fixed up on a date with your Great Aunt Louise's friend's grandson, especially after hearing what a "clean-cut young man" he is. In your experience, "clean-cut young man" either means (a) boring-as-sin alphabetizer of DMV surcharge documents whose idea of fun is combing the beach with a metal detector, (b) serial killer who has cleared space in his freezer for you, or (c) both of the above.

Well, at least the guy didn't kill you—yet—but after one date, you are absolutely positive you never want to see him again. You haven't exactly spelled this out, but you would think that your refusal to take or return any of his fifty-seven phone calls might have implied this. However, as good as he might be at detecting metal, this guy is not very good at detecting "no."

It's too bad you don't have a device that can detect him, because if you did, you never would've ventured to the grocery store today. Because who should you see, weirdly weighing individual eggs on the produce scale, but Mr. Not-So-Right. At the very moment you try to duck, he spots you and makes a beeline in your direction. You make a desperate attempt to run, but he's stunningly fast and agile, and he blocks your way with his cart. You are so busted.

Don't Act Guilty

The truth is, you've been totally avoiding this person, and now you've been caught. But the last I checked, avoiding a person who's totally annoying and can't take "no" for an answer is not a punishable crime. So ease up on your guilt! It's great that you're a nice person and you don't like to hurt people, but sometimes, there's really no other choice. This guy already has you where he wants you (literally trapped by his grocery cart) and if you let him guilt you, he'll also have you where he wants you psychologically, too. See, people who glom onto other people—I call them "social parasites"—are a very hearty breed. They *know* that other people don't want them around, and they've developed elaborate ways to force themselves into your life anyway. Guilt is one of their key survival techniques. If you act too flustered and give way to guilt, he will be holding all the cards.

Busy, Busy

One of the first things you should say is that you've been really busy lately, whether or not it is true. You've been busy avoiding him, haven't you? If you want, you can even pull the guilt-reversal technique, wherein you say, "Yes, I've had a family emergency that has kept me busy." This turns the guilt right back on him! How dare he act so confrontational, given what you've been dealing with!? Another great option is the "personal crisis." This works on a few levels: It takes the guilt off you, and also draws a clear line between your personal life and this guy. If he tries to get more information out of you, very politely say that you'd rather not discuss it. A lot of us "nice girls" don't know the line between being courteous and having no boundaries at all. You can do one without doing the other.

Avoid C. A. G. E.

Another pitfall "nice girls" run into, when confronted by someone they've been avoiding, is pressure to make future plans. You're trapped, you're guilty and embarrassed, and they're saying, "When can we hang out?" You feel as though the only way you can escape is to agree to a future plan. But this will only perpetuate the vicious cycle of Calls, Avoidance, Guilt, and Entrapment (C. A. G. E. for short. Yes, I made that up). Say something vague, like, "It would be nice to see you again (a lie, yes), but I'm swamped right now." This is unlikely to slake the insatiable appetite of the social parasite, but unless they want to look totally deranged in public, they have to accept it. All that's left is to say, "It was nice to see you," and run.

An Accent to Get Noticed at the Bar

You and your friends are at the bar, looking amazing, and yet for some ridiculous reason, you are not attracting the level of attention appropriate to your gorgeousness. Maybe it's the fact that this place is crawling with women, sadly desperate women who seem to have no qualms about showing ever-increasing amounts of cleavage and inviting guys to do tequila shots off their stomachs. You and your friends would rather not compete on that level, but being ignored in this manner is unacceptable.

Then one of you comes up with the idea: Let's fake accents! At first you laugh, but then her bizarre logic starts to make sense. The exoticness of a beautiful woman who is also foreign might just trump body shots, especially since those girls look like they're about to pass out any minute now. Yes, you might lose out on the guys who prefer their women mute and unconscious, but hopefully, that's not your type!

The Drunken Accent

One of the most effective accents to fake at this point is the "drunken accent." True, it doesn't necessarily add to your exotic foreignness, but it shows that you are currently a citizen of the Nation of Inebriation. The drunken accent is subtle but involves the slurring together of words, increased loudness, and the declaration to your friends that, "I just love you *so* much!" The best part about faking a drunken accent is that guys might think this makes you particularly easy targets, but you know better. You can maintain a clear head and the upper hand, but your accent will make you, what I will call "approachable." While the other *truly* drunken women in this place are dropping like flies, you and your friends will be fake-slurring the night away!

French Kiss

One of the most exotic—and sexy—accents to fake is a French accent. Really, there's no guy alive who wouldn't want to say he seduced a French girl. And hey—the French were the ones who gave us the word "faux," so they must be cool with us faking their accent, right?

There are a few things to remember when faking a French accent. According to writers at *www.wikihow.com*, your pronunciation of the "r" is one of the most fundamental rules of fake Frenchiness. When pronouncing the "r," you should push your tongue to the back of your mouth. What comes out should sound like a rolling "gr" type of sound. It might feel or sound awkward, but it's the way they do it! Another trick is to pronounce the "i" as a short vowel sound, like you would a double "e"—so "dish" would be pronounced "deesh." The English "th" combination should be changed to a "dz" combination. So, "this" would be pronounced "deezs." Finally, *www.wikihow.com* advises stressing the last syllable of a sentence, and ending the sentence like you're asking a question. So, you might say, "I have never been to deezs bagrrr?"

Because, in your faux French role, you aren't entirely comfortable with English, you can limit your words and act shy. And hey, even if your French accent isn't perfect, you can always assure him that your kisses speak perfect French!

The Madonna Accent

Probably the easiest accent for us Americans to fake is British. This might be because we share the same language, and it might be because we have Madonna to look to for tips. Madge, who is British by way of Detroit, takes on an exaggeratedly clipped enunciation and says things like, "I ab-solutely *loathe* hydrangeas," or "That's really rubbish, isn't it?" You should also drop the "r" at the end of words, but not in the middle of words, and add a lot of "bloodies," "loves," and "mates."

Warning: Americans tend to view British people as being very intelligent, cultured and aloof, and this might not be the impression you want to give if you're out at a bar with American guys. That's why the Madonna accent is so important. She might try to sound classy, but nobody thinks she's even remotely "like a virgin." Cheers!

Holding Your Own During the Holidays

You love your life: You've worked hard to get out of your hometown, establish a career, buy a house, and make great friends. You're a confident, intelligent, accomplished woman who works hard, is the life of the party, and is deserving of love and respect. You're attractive. You haven't had a bad perm for literally years.

These are just some of the affirmations you will need to say to yourself in order to survive going home—or even to an isolated family function—for the holidays.

It's always the same: At first, you look forward to getting there, telling them about the recent developments in your life, relating to them as a fellow adult. Then you get there, and as far as they're concerned, you're still the twelve-year-old in the peach-colored '80s glasses and a sweatshirt with a wolf on it. They listen to you pretending to be a grownup for about ten minutes, then your cousin Jimmy gives you an Indian rope burn and calls you "Spazz," his old nickname for you. Your dad asks if you've let your car run out of gas lately (a bad habit from your youth), and your Aunt Marie asks if you're *still single* as if she were asking if you *still have malaria*.

"Aw, it's nice to see ya, Spazz," cousin Jimmy says. Some things never change. But wait—*you've* changed! Why can't your family see that?

Bring Souvenirs from Your Real Life

Families suffer from a kind of collective poor vision—all they can see are the designated family roles they established years ago. So if you're the family nerd, the loser, or the spazz, their tendency will be to see that—even if you have three doctorate degrees and have won the Nobel Prize.

One strategy I find useful when visiting family is to bring a souvenir from your *real* life. This can be anything that reminds you of your current life and who you really are, which is very different from the outdated memories your family might still maintain. Best of all is a human souvenir, like a good friend who doesn't want to see her family, either. If you can't bring a person, try to have a friend on hand to talk to on the phone or by text, just to give you reminders that you are understood, valued, and highly regarded as a fully adult human being. Or, if you're in a pinch, just bring your Nobel Prize along for the trip.

Don't Try to "Sell" Yourself

One trap grown children fall into during the holidays is to try to "sell" the new, mature version of themselves to their family members. This isn't necessary or helpful. Families are quite resistant to updating their ideas of who you are now. If you were a little kid with pigtails, Great Aunt Edna might not be able to accommodate your current identity as a political activist and roller derby queen. No matter. It's not important. You don't need to convince Great Aunt Edna of anything, no more than she needs to convince you that her nose hair is not a living creature.

Try Not to Be Hurt

It's possible that someone in your family might say something hurtful about your current life. Maybe Uncle George will say, "Well, I thought you had more sense than to try to open a *dog bakery* during a recession. What is a dog bakery? Do you bake dogs?" or "Hmm, so your boyfriend is a musician. Does that mean he's unemployed?" Or, "Oh, so you're a vegetarian. Doesn't that kind of conflict with your dog bakery?" There is really no end to the things family members might try to say, especially if your lifestyle seems threatening or opposed to their way of life. I would advise returning to the mantra that, "My life is good. This isn't my real life. This is a bizarre suspended reality known as the holidays." And it will be over, and you'll survive it. You want to project a quiet dignity, a sort of "I'm past all your nonsense" aura. It really is a wonderful life. Honest!

A Date So Your Friends Stop Setting You Up with the Guys in Their Lives

Your friends might mean well, but things usually don't end well when people "mean well." The phrase, "mean well," is nothing but a preface to disastrous behavior committed with nice intentions. In fact, just FYI, if someone ever says to you, "I know you mean well," you can expect a big "but" and an explanation of what you did that sort of sucked.

Okay, now that I've finished that rant, let's talk about your well-meaning friends. The trouble is, they set you up with each and every male human who crosses their paths: their weird brothers, guys they rejected, the undertakers at their grandma's funerals. They set you up with their secretly married plumbers, and their secretly gay yoga instructors. You're pretty sure they're one step away from setting you up with their dogs and their robotic vacuum cleaners.

It's gotten pretty insulting, actually. Clearly, your one friend thinks you're not above dating a bald, sixty-five-year-old taxidermist she found selling stuffed alligators at a roadside stand, and another imagines you might be fine with a convicted car thief who "only has a few more months" before his release.

You can't take this anymore. Something has to change, and that something is your relationship status. You have to fake a date—and an amazing one, ASAP.

Get a Text Boyfriend

To plant the initial seed of your new relationship status, you need to start getting texts from your fake man. To this end, there are a few "fake boyfriend" services available online. For a set fee, you can get a set number of sweet, attentive and charming texts from this faux beau per week. If your friends ask who this mysterious texting man is, you can say, "He's somebody special I've been seeing," and make a face that is both enigmatic and quite pleased. If they ask whether it's serious, you can lay the groundwork by saying, "Let's just put it this way: I don't think I'm going to need to be set up on any blind dates anytime soon."

Have a Long Distance Love

Here's one problem with the text boyfriend—if this guy is important enough to call a halt to all fix-ups, your friends will probably expect him to become an in-person fixture. And unless you know some guy who is willing to play that role on an ongoing basis, your best faking option is probably a long-distance relationship.

Say you met this guy on a work trip, or visiting a relative, or even online if necessary. He'll have to live far enough away to justify his infrequent visits. Or, you can say that when he does manage to come to town, he wants to maximize his time alone with you. Aw, I like this guy already!

If you can't get a friend or coworker to pose as your man for an evening, what you will probably need to do is hire an amateur actor. Often, you can find guys who do singing telegrams, or even strippers, for local companies. Offer to pay them the same amount they would get for an "event" to pretend to be your boyfriend. Surely, they can show up to your friend's party, look handsome, and answer a few basic questions. If you happen to hire a stripper, remind him that he does not need to take off his clothes. Although if he does, that might put an end to all the questions!

Be Ready to Dump Him

Yes, this fake man—let's call him "George Glass"—is serving a valuable purpose for you right now, by keeping your friends' hideous setups at bay. But should you meet someone special, you need to be willing to dump this dude immediately, even if your friends love him. You need to tell them George cheated on you with a bisexual clown prostitute. And got her pregnant. And gave you gonorrhea—whatever it takes to get out of your fake relationship and into a real one.

CHAPTER THREE

Charming Your Prince

"Just Be Yourself." This is the simplistic, rose-colored advice your mom, friends and other supporters give you when you're about to go on a first date. What they don't tell you is that this advice comes with more small-print disclaimers than a Viagra commercial (by the way, "Call your doctor for any erection lasting more than four hours" is sound advice for any life situation). Basically, you should be yourself *unless* yourself happens to be insecure, needy, desirous of a husband and/or children, burdened with a colorful sexual history, apathetic to sports, uninterested in video games, inclined to go to the bathroom, and unable to have an orgasm on cue. If "yourself" just so happens to be free of any of the above flaws, by all means, be that person. Otherwise, you might have to tone down those aspects of yourself until he's fallen madly and irreversibly in love with you.

Women get a bad reputation for presenting a "sham" self to guys in order to snag them for marriage. In reality, both genders hold back their less-than-wonderful traits in the beginning in order to make a good impression. If we didn't fake it a bit in the beginning, how would anyone ever get past the first date? If anything, we just have different motives. Women fake to avoid hurting a guy's feelings or to not appear desperate for a long-term relationship. Guys fake it to get you into bed. Or, as the lovely Sharon Stone said, "Women might be able to fake orgasms, but men can fake whole relationships." So don't feel too bad about a little bit of strategic concealment, ladies—they don't call it "the battle of the sexes" for nothing!

An Orgasm When It's Never Going to Happen

Like most of us women, I'm sure you've been there—in bed with a guy, waiting for the Big Moment to occur, reaching for it like the brass ring on the Merry-Go-Round, and realizing that it is cruelly eluding you. No matter how long you stay on the ride, it's just not going to be a very "merry" go-round this time.

It could be that you're stressed, or tired, or have your mind on other things (unlike guys, women have trouble enjoying sex when their lives are falling apart all around them—we're weird like that). Or maybe you're with a guy who is so clueless he thinks the "G-spot" is a section of the parking garage at the mall.

Either way, you've missed your window this time, and you're ready to wrap it up and call it a night. But your partner seems to be courteously waiting for your "big finish" before he concludes his business. If he wants a real orgasm, he could be waiting a really long time. It's like he's politely holding the door for you at the supermarket when you haven't even left your house yet. It's enough to make you wish that chivalry were dead.

If, however, you can perform a convincing piece of theater, the two of you could be happily drifting off to dreamland within ten minutes. It's not exactly Shakespeare, but it could be the role of your lifetime!

Porn: A Faker's Best Friend

The truth is, the pornography industry has done a lot of the groundwork in terms of making your guy gullible in this regard. You know how kids become desensitized to movie explosions and shootouts? Well, so do adult men become desensitized to over-the-top, loud moaning, screaming, and "Oh, God" and "Oh, yeah!"-ing. Guys usually watch a lot more porn than women. What might strike you as preposterously overdone may, therefore, seem entirely credible to him. These imaginary scenarios, combined with their natural egos, have led them to think that women really do reach those levels of ecstasy every single time.

My point is, although I do think it's best not to overact while faking orgasm, you do have a fairly wide range to work with. Do what you are most comfortable doing—this is the best way to make your performance believable.

Build Up Gradually

According to a video tutorial from *www.howcast.com*, the most convincing fake orgasm is one where you let your "excitement" build up gradually. Allow your breathing to become more irregular and ragged, and let out moans of increasing intensity and volume. If you're not big into the loud moan, that's okay, but just allow yourself to gradually sound more urgent and excited. Remember, this is supposed to be an involuntary thing, so don't make the moans too regular or perfectly timed, or they might seem fake. Another good approach is to close your eyes, since this is often what you'd do if it were real (plus, looking him right in the eye while faking might be too big of a challenge).

Reach the Crescendo

As you get closer to your grand finale, allow more and more involuntary reactions to take place. The writers at *www.howcast.com* recommend perhaps biting your lip, or tensing your muscles in your legs or feet. Your body might twitch a bit (don't overdo this, as might seem like you're having a seizure) or you might call out his name or some other preferred exclamation (not someone else's name though, okay?). Grabbing onto something, such as a pillow or his hair, is a nice touch to signal your imminent delight. Then give a loud gasp—gasping is good—and maybe a moan if you'd like, letting it last a few seconds, then relax your body. You can laugh, sigh, or kiss him—some bit of punctuation to let him know you're done. What's best is, he probably won't be capable of critical analysis of your performance, because he'll be right behind you with his own big finish. Believe me, this will wipe out everything else, including, occasionally, his ability to call you by the correct name. Oops!

Interest in Your Partner's Favorite Sports Team

It's that season again—let's just call it *boyfriend season*—when you are called upon to pretend to enjoy watching sports and participating in "jock culture."

Whether it's football, baseball, basketball, or that sport with the flying broomsticks they play in "Harry Potter" (actually, if your man is into this, you might not have to worry about jock culture), your man's obsession with his sport of choice probably rivals his obsession with you. This, really, is kind of annoying—the only brawny men in tight pants who should ever be a threat to you are the rogue pirates in your swashbuckling hijack fantasy.

Nevertheless, the fine tradition of men and sports probably dates all the way back to the Roman Empire, when wives were rumored to have complained, "Oh, you and your gladiator games with your precious buddies. God forbid I should ask you to stay home and watch little Ovid while *my* friends and I go get our fortunes read through bird guts."

Do you want to be that complaining harpy? No. Rather than competing with the sport, you want to embrace it, so your man will embrace you. Once you win him over for keeps, you can drop this whole façade and go back to watching HGTV. But for now, you need to fake being a fan.

Dress the Part

As a female, you'll find that one potentially enjoyable part of being a faux sports fan is to assemble your sporty wardrobe. Blogger Allison James at *www.chicksareweird.com* calls the look of the female fan "drunk-at-a-sports-bar chic." For this I recommend a casual but deliberate look—tight, low-rise jeans that, from a barstool perspective, reveal your temporary lower-back tattoo of his team.

Also, a jersey for his team is a great idea. Don't worry about having to wear some hideous color—they make jerseys for all teams in pink these days, just for us girly fans. They also make fitted little baby tees and ringer tees for women whose interest in sports is aimed mostly at scoring that man.

When choosing a jersey, you also have to decide which player you want represented on your back. This is easy—just pick the hottest guy on the team who is also skilled at football. This will not only show that you're an awesome sport but will no doubt make your man jealous. Well done!

Play the "Fantasy" Version of His Game

As ridiculous as it may sound, you can also worm your way into his sports-loving heart by participating in fantasy league play. By doing this, you can learn some important sports terms, endear yourself to his friends with good-natured trash talking, and really lock in his affections. You guys could even play a secret little "fantasy" game, where every time a player on his fantasy team scores, *he* scores. This will create a Pavlovian association between sports and your sexy self, allowing you to infiltrate (and maybe even replace) sports in his mind. Touchdown!

Let the Other Ladies Know

Okay, so you've transformed yourself into a jersey-wearing, beer-swilling, fantasy sports-playing chick. That's great, but you should be prepared to get some dirty looks from your fellow women. For many of us, a sports-loving woman is a traitor to our gender. So expect appalled stares from the wives of your man's friends as you jock it up with the guys over Buffalo wings. They'll roll their eyes and saunter away in their nonsporty stilettos, leaving you with three belching men and a fourth guy's name on your back.

"Wait!" You want to scream. "This isn't really me! I'm just doing this to lock in that guy! Come *back*!"

This type of confusion is exactly why I think there should be some international signal for sports fakery between women. Here's what I propose—a cheap replica of a Super Bowl ring, worn on the engagement ring finger. This will symbolize that sports are merely a strategy, a placeholder for the lifetime commitment you seek. Once you get that other ring, this Super Bowl ring will come off like a prom dress. Or, more specifically, like a wedding dress.

A Good Date When It's the Worst One You've Been On

WTF!? Could this date possibly get any worse? First, the guy shows up at the restaurant wearing a wife-beater, skinny jeans and fluorescent green crocs. You try to look past these heinous fashion crimes as you imbibe a pre-dinner glass of wine. As the alcohol enters your system, you start to enjoy his sense of humor, which isn't excellent, but at least it exists. He also has a nice smile and earns points by saying he doesn't really go clubbing anymore—he's more of a "homebody" these days. It's almost enough to make you forgive the crocs.

Then your eyes scan up from the offending foam resin shoes to reveal a disturbing accessory—an electronic ankle bracelet. Before you even have time to ask about this, he tells you that he "escaped" his house arrest to come out on this date, and that if he doesn't get home soon, he's probably going to jail. Couldn't you give him a ride home? He'd love to continue the date at his house.

Again, WTF!? Although this is certainly the most creative approach any guy has taken to lure you back to his house, it's also the worst. Especially since you haven't even ordered dinner and he's not making a move to pick up the drink tab. Meanwhile, the clock is running out on House Arrest Cinderella here. And those crocs are a far cry from "magic slippers." A "homebody," indeed!

Had a Great Time

Okay, so it goes without saying that you're never going to see this man again, except maybe on a "wanted" poster. You just want to end the night with a minimum of drama. As you walk him to the cab you plan to put him in, try to say something sort of nice, since these are hopefully the last words you will ever utter to him. Feel free to employ some humor. Say, "Well, it was a short date, but certainly an adventure. It was nice to meet you." If he tries to get you to commit to another date, you can say something vague, like, "Well, things are looking really busy right now . . . I'm sure I'll see you around." This is a white lie to get you out of this situation. And hey, you might see him sometime, when you are required to testify against him at his parole violation hearing.

No Guilt!

It is very important that you not reveal any guilt over the fact that you hated this date and never want to see this person again. Guilt is the kiss of death when you are trying to lose a loser. If he senses you are a little bit of a pushover, he will try to play that for all it's worth. You don't owe this guy anything. You can mention a few positive aspects of the date—were there any? Oh, right, you did like his sense of humor there for a minute, unless it was just the wine. But don't say, "I liked your sense of humor;" that's too personal. Cite one funny story he told and say, "Oh, I liked that story of your experience bartering cigarettes and shanks with your friends, ha-ha."

No Kiss!

If guilt is the kiss of death, then a kiss is the kiss of worse-than-death, and the only thing worse than death would be to get stuck in a relationship with this guy. Under no circumstances are you obligated to kiss this person. You can be nice, mildly complimentary, and generically polite, but you don't need to make contact with his lips. If he tries to go in for the kiss, you're going to have to turn your head and give him the infamous mouth full of hair. Honestly, if you've suffered through a bad date, you should not further need to suffer through a bad kiss, too. I would suggest politely shaking his hand. You can allow a peck only if there seems to be absolutely no way to avoid it in a socially acceptable way. Just remember that it's a kiss goodbye.

Past Adventures and Stories to Entertain Your Date

You've always loved a good story and have always admired those people who can spin an awesome tale in a social situation or on a date. You've noticed how people gravitate toward these great storytellers, these conjurers of humor, drama and even magic out of the ridiculousness of everyday life. You want to *be* that person, the one who commands the spotlight, who has people hanging on your every word—especially that hot guy at your office with his big brown eyes. You want him hanging on your words like they're a jungle gym and he's Tarzan.

Yet your life story, up until now, has really been pretty boring. You haven't done much. You were born, went to school, made friends, had a few boyfriends, went to college, and went to work. Not exactly the stuff of a miniseries or a standup routine, is it?

Okay, before you concoct elaborate tales about the time you wrestled an alligator or climbed Mount Everest with James Franco, you should stop and think about this. Are you writing a check that your past can't cash?

Keep It Clean

One mistake you *don't* want to make on a date is to tell detailed stories of your freewheeling adventures on the singles or bar scene. While you and your friends might crack up every time you tell the story about the time you unknowingly made out in the dark with a guy who had an outbreak of lip herpes, this will be exponentially less endearing to a prospective boyfriend. Nobody wants to hear about someone's crazy hookups, especially not on the first or second date. In the beginning, wild stories about your romantic past basically telegraph that you are unpredictable, possibly immature, and worst of all—not relationship material. This might be a totally unfair portrayal of you, but sadly, that's what gets reflected if you plunge right in with stories that sound like a special edition of *Girls Gone Wild*. Sorry, I didn't make the rules!

Listen to Him, Too!

You might long to be the awesome storytelling queen, but don't forget that guys often love to tell stories, too. In fact, you might find yourself on a date with a guy who has stories so crazy they make yours sound like you're reading aloud from the phone book. In fact, wouldn't it be hilarious if he made up a bunch of preposterous stories, too? Having entirely made-up lives could be kind of exciting for a while—it would be like your whole relationship was part of the witness protection program! Except you guys never actually witnessed anything—just eight-hour workdays, boring parties, and shopping excursions at the Gap.

You never know, though—he might just have some genuinely intriguing stories! So why not hear him out? There's nothing wrong with occasionally being the audience instead of the star.

Use Other People's Lives

You might not realize it, but you do have stories worth telling. They're called other people's lives. You just have to learn to tell them well. If you're talking about Thanksgiving with your family, don't talk about the menu items or the weather—talk about crazy Aunt Bea and her obsession with hand sanitizer or your cousin Fred and the end-of-the-world bunker he's building. Most likely, all you have to do is think of the people in your life—family, friends, coworkers—and you're going to think of some pretty crazy behaviors to talk about. There's that coworker who has written in her will that she wants to be made into a diamond to be put on her dog's collar or that guy who has been telling people he has "heart cancer." Other people's lives add wonderful material to mine and present like the little nuggets of gold they are. You might feel like a terrible gossip, but it's better to be a gossip than to risk being caught fabricating your entire life. Unless your crazy lies are so huge you get to go on *Oprah* to confess them.

A Laugh When Your Partner's Jokes Are Far from Funny

Aside from prancing around in sexy lingerie and cooking delicious food, what's the top advice you see for women on how to win the heart of a guy? If you guessed *laugh at his jokes,* you win. Your prize? Lots of really stupid jokes to laugh at. Enjoy!

The male ego, from what we've learned about it thus far, seems to be wrapped up in a few things: sexual prowess, success at work, and a sense of humor. For whatever reason, being funny is an important part of being a man. Yet, trying to laugh at a totally unfunny joke is like being told to feel amazingly wonderful when your hand touches a hot stove. It's just not natural. And some of the worst fake laughs I've ever heard have been those polite, sickly sweet, overdone laughs of women (my own included). What does a man's fake laugh even sound like? Does anyone even know? Probably not, because laughter isn't one of the things guys fake. They're more worried about pretending they're going to call you or faking not having a thing for your best friend. Yay! Now there's a joke to laugh at!

Put Your Hand over Your Mouth

According to editors at *www.wikihow.com*, clamping a hand over your mouth, while pretending to laugh, is a useful technique and will increase the believability of your fake laugh. Not sure why, except that maybe covering your mouth hides the fact that you're actually scowling? Probably, too, the hand-over-the-mouth trick muffles some of the phony, high-pitched abrasiveness of the fake-girl laugh. Also, if you are about to vomit over the stupidity of his joke, covering your mouth might conceal that to some degree as well. So the hand-over-the-mouth method can serve as a catchall. Literally.

Laugh at Your Own Jokes, Too

If you use your fake laugh to punctuate your own jokes, too, then your guy will be more likely to believe it is real. Of course, he'll then think of you as a person who laughs at your own jokes, but hey, *someone* ought to laugh at them! You're a funny girl!

The idea is, if you use the same laugh for your own jokes that you use for his, it's got to be legit. It's sort of like the notion that if you serve yourself coffee from the same pot that you serve his from, there's less likely to be arsenic in it. Be careful, though—sometimes your jokes are quite good, and you might catch yourself unleashing a genuine guffaw or two for yourself. He'll recognize the contrast between real and fake right away.

Get a Laugh Track

Remember those laugh tracks from old sitcoms? They were cues that people were supposed to laugh—which, when you think about it, must mean the jokes were pretty lame. What you can do is get him a laugh track, which he can activate when he's told a joke or just when he wants to enter the room in a funny way like Lenny and Squiggy on *Laverne & Shirley*. When he pushes the laugh button, you will know that it is time for you to also laugh. If you don't quite hit the mark, all of those other people laughing will make him feel a ton better. And maybe, if it's needed, you can get a live studio audience "applause track" for his, ahem, intimate performances. He'll feel like he's been inducted into the Bedroom Hall of Fame! Just be careful you don't hit the laugh button by mistake.

Being Drunk When You Text That Guy You Just Started Dating

So you just started dating this guy, and from what you can tell so far, he's pretty awesome. You've only been on a few dates, but you've had some unforgettable kisses and some fun conversations. He's handsome, smart, entertaining, seemingly stable—all of that. Right now, you are smitten.

You're not going to be seeing him for a while, though, because he's away visiting family out of state. The absence is just making your heart grow fonder, and you want to take advantage of the distance to send him some fun, flirty little "thinking of you" texts. What you really want is to say, "OMG, I love you, I have been trying on your last name all night long, how many children do you want?" but in your experience, this tends to scare guys away. As it is, even your little flirty stuff is a bit risky, since it's so early on and you don't know where you stand. For this reason, you want to reserve the right to retract your statements in the morning. Therefore, you need to pretend to be just a little bit drunk. If you claim to be drunk, your little lapses into sappiness will actually seem very restrained. You will seem like a very composed, dignified drunk girl.

Get a Sixty-Something to Compose the Texts for You

One great way to signify drunkenness while texting is to commit many typographical and spelling errors. You're a whiz at texting though, so you'd probably have to try really hard to spell things wrong. This is why you have to get a person who is at least sixty years of age (fifty to fifty-five will do if you are desperate) to type your texts for you. A person within these age ranges will be bewildered and baffled by "how small the keys are" and will repeatedly exclaim, "I don't know how you kids do it." Just dictate everything you want to say to this elder person, and they will naturally misspell every third word or so. Even better, they will take so long to type a reply that your guy might momentarily worry that you died. Thus, when he finally receives your answer, he will be overjoyed that you are still among the living. "Wow, she must really be wasted if she's taking this long to reply," he'll think. Nope, you're just chilling out at the AARP headquarters!

Disable Autocorrect

Okay, although autocorrect certainly has the potential to add to the illusion that you are drunk, I'm not sure you would want to make the kinds of mistakes it tends to make—especially with a senior citizen at the helm of your phone. Autocorrect has a very dirty mind and tends to create typos that are both perverse and embarrassing. So even if it says something a little bit racy, it's probably not going to be a good kind of racy. According to *www.damnyouautocorrect.com*, you might accidentally find yourself saying that you "need some new penises—mine broke" or that you "love oblong wieners."

Basically, these are funny mistakes, but they might not be the kind of thing you would want to say to a guy you're just getting to know. You could be so embarrassed you might not even be able to face him the next day, as you struggle with your fake hangover.

Be a Little More Playful

Really, it's very easy to pretend to be drunk while texting. Because your physical self isn't involved, you don't have to change your tone, you don't have to slur your words, and you don't have to be wobbly when you walk. All you have to do is seem just a little bit less inhibited and a little bit more honest. If you sense later that he wasn't ready for this level of playfulness or flirtation, you can always retreat by saying you were tipsy and no harm done. But maybe he will flirt right back—and maybe he will be drunk for real, which will really help. Hey, why not have a drink yourself, while you're at it?

An Incoming Call When a Date Goes Bad

You're on a date that started out iffy, then progressed to not so good, and then took a rapid nosedive to absolutely horrific. This guy's versions of "compliments" to you are that he "likes a girl with meat on her bones," "likes a woman who's not too intellectual," and "likes a girl who's not so pretty she's a snob." Despite the fact that his compliments have more backhand than a Serena Williams tennis game, he's now pawing ineptly at you like a raccoon trying to knock over a trash can. Oh, and apparently he likes a girl who picks up the check, too.

He's proposed the idea that you hang out and have some more drinks, and maybe go back to his place, but you're pretty sure you'd rather be skinned alive. But then he'd have access to all that *meat on your bones,* and you wouldn't want to give him the satisfaction. Come on, now—you don't need to put up with this crap, not even for another minute. You know what time it is, right? It's half-past time to fake an incoming phone call.

The Emergency Text

Back in the days before cell phones, people had to rely on the most archaic methods for getting out of bad dates, like having a friend actually show up at the date location with some "emergency." Imagine how difficult that was back in the days before cars existed—the date intervener had to hitch up the horse and buggy and drive for days, by which time the date was probably over. It's no wonder so many people in olden days ended up marrying people they hated—no one showed up to get them out of it!

Now all of our fancy little gadgets make it easier than ever to end a horrendous date. In particular, our cell phones are little miracles of faux emergency.

There are a wide variety of options for using your cell phone in this way, ranging from the homemade approach to actual paid services. The most basic approach would be the emergency text, wherein you pretend to get a text calling you away from your date immediately. Of course, you can arrange to get a real text from a participating friend at a set time, or you can text your friend a code requesting this text. You can even show your emergency text to the guy—if it's right there in writing that your grandpa's in the hospital, it can't be a lie, can it? If you do show the guy your friend's text, though, make sure he doesn't see her phone number. She really wouldn't appreciate having this freak calling her, either!

There's an App . . .

Yes, we have reached a point in our civilization where we're simultaneously more technologically savvy and more socially inept than ever. It makes sense, then, that at this juncture we would have at our disposal services whereby we can pay to have a date-interrupting phone call made to our cell phones.

There are actually several different apps out there for putting a horrible date out of its misery. You can arrange to get a work-related phone call, a request from a friend to bail him out of jail, or an emergency summons to the hospital. As I previously mentioned, one service even lets you get a phone call from a famous person, which will show up on your caller ID! You can get a call from the president! Why would you want to stick around this weirdo when you have celebrities to see?

Not Being Crazy When You First Meet a Man

You have a lot going for you—you're smart, funny, adorable and caring. You have a great job, a nice apartment, a killer wardrobe and a bright future. The only problem? You're completely and totally insane.

That's right—crazy! Especially when it comes to dating. You've had a few bad experiences, and they have made you, unfortunately, into a neurotic, paranoid, high- maintenance mess. You don't trust that a guy is ever where he says he is, even if he's sitting right in front of you. You get jealous if a guy you're dating talks to the waitress—even if all he's saying is, "I'd like the spaghetti" and the waitress is his mom. You made your last boyfriend call twice a day, plus a third time just to talk to your cat. Sadly, you drove him away. Your cat misses him.

And despite your utter distrust of men, you are absolutely, totally desperate to snag one of them for marriage and reproduction. Like, yesterday.

All of this tends to ooze out of you like oil out of a teenager's skin. You scare more guys away than an all-day Katherine Heigl film festival. They look at you, and they see someone who wants to entrap them, torture them, and force them to go antiquing. You have to shut down this crazy vibe, or else you're never going to be able to get your hooks into some poor, unsuspecting victim.

Discuss Your Interests

When you first meet a guy, you want him to see that you have other interests besides simply capturing a marriageable guy, utilizing his genetic material to make offspring, and mounting his head on your wall like a ten-point buck. Seeming too transparently focused on your not-so-hidden agenda will seem absolutely bat-crap wacko. Being passionate about other things—hobbies, your job, volunteer work, your friends—shows that you're a well-rounded and interesting person. If you don't have any other interests, I suggest you take a dating hiatus and find some. Yes, you might think, "That's a waste of valuable man-snagging time," but I would argue that this is time better spent than time spent dating with that crazed, obsessively eager look in your eye.

A few interests/hobbies you should *not* mention:

- Taking high doses of prenatal vitamins
- Semi-professional bride bouquet catching
- Finding a "new daddy" for your cat
- Embryo photography

Speed Date

If you're crazy and would prefer to wait a while before you show it, an excellent approach for you is the speed date. This will expose you to many, many eligible guys for very short, insanity-limiting periods of time. The numbers are definitely in your favor.

The first thing you need to do when preparing for a speed dating session is to make sure you look absolutely smoking hot. Just a hint of sexy will drive a guy to distraction. And that's what you want—distraction from the fact that you are nuts.

On each speed date, don't go too crazy talking. Answer questions about what you do for a living, where you live, what you like to do. Be sure to avoid mentioning how often you drive past your ex's house or the fact that this guy's "speed dates" with the other women in the room constitute cheating in your book.

Double Date

Another way to minimize your craziness is to ask a good girlfriend of yours to help you deceive this poor sucker. She knows how nuts you are, too, but what are friends for, if not to trick hapless guys into marrying you?

Have her and her significant other (or just some guy *she* wants to trick into marriage) come out for a double date with you and your guy. Have her rave about you all night, emphasizing how awesome and not certifiable you are. Make sure you monitor the guys at all times, though—men sometimes have secret signals to let each other know a chick is crazy. You can't allow that. Not when you're this close. Why, you'd rather kill someone and discreetly dump his body in the river than let that happen!

Your Relationship History When You've Done (or Haven't Done) Things You're Not Proud Of

So, it's gotten to that point in your relationship known as the "confessional stage." You've declared love for one another, and you spend your magical days gazing into each other's eyes, marveling at how lucky you are to have found each other. In fact, you two are so in love, it's hard to even imagine the other having a life (and loves!) before you.

"So, what about the guys before me?" he asks dreamily. "Tell me all about it. I want to know everything about you."

Uh-oh. This is a tough one. Guys claim they want to know all about your sexual past, but really, they only want to know stuff that will make them feel better (we're the same way, by the way). You want to be entirely honest, since you're pouring your hearts out to one another, but you suspect there are a few things in your past that would be best kept under wraps. Or alternately, you are worried that your relative lack of experience in the sexual category could make you seem incredibly boring. How do you fake your history without sounding shady and secretive, *or* without overdoing it?

Men Need to Win

Here is a crucial piece of male psychology that should guide you in faking your sexual history: When it comes to sex, *men need to win.* According to *www.goodmenproject.com*, the reason guys get so freaked out when a woman has had a lot of sexual partners is because that means more competition. If he's only competing against five people, he's more likely to rank number one than if he's competing with fifty. For reasons that are not entirely known but might have something to do with all those competing sperm for that one egg, sex is a game guys need to win.

So when fabricating your sexual past, whether it's on the higher end or the lower end, remember that your current guy needs to be Number One. That's why, in general, I think it's more to your benefit to play your number down rather than play it up. Either way, though, you will need to convince him, like Mirror, Mirror on the Wall, that he is the most potent, long lasting and pleasure giving of them all. If you even so much as insinuate that another guy outperformed him, you will never, ever be allowed to forget about this for the rest of your life.

Skip the Details

For the reasons described above, I would not go into details about your sexual past, unless they happen to be details that make your previous lovers seem like incompetent oafs. You can tell a funny story about the guy who wore a prosthetic penis in his pants or the guy who thought you would like it if he slathered you in Thousand Island salad dressing. But details about stuff that you actually enjoyed should be kept mum. Even if your guy says he's trying to find out what you like, that's not the route to go in telling him. Guys are fairly persistent about this, so be on guard. He might say something like, "Come on, there must have been some guy who knew how to give you what you wanted." Just smile mysteriously and say, "Not like you do," and give him a big kiss. He's the big winner!

Careful with the Experiments

Guys might also press to find out about other crazy things you've done, such as experimentation with other girls or threesomes. Unless he seems like a very open-minded guy, I would refrain from discussing any such thing. However, some guys genuinely do enjoy the idea of their woman being a little bit kinky, particularly when it comes to bi-curious adventures. If you think your man is this kind of guy, feel free to give him information in small doses and see how he takes it. The point you want to get across to him is that even if he's not your first, you want him to be your last. Winner takes all!

Liking Your Partner's Family

You've been dating your guy for about six months now, and you know he's The One. You've gotten through the first date awkwardness, the conceal-your-insecurities phase, and the okay-you-can-see-me-without-makeup phase, and he has passed each test with flying colors. Even better, he is totally in love with you, too: He even thinks it's adorable when you have PMS and cry into your Heath Bar Crunch ice cream. You know, almost without a doubt, that you are going to stay with this man for the rest of your life. After meeting his family, though, you're starting to hope that the rest of your life will be mercifully short.

Seriously, this family is truly a can of mixed nuts. His mom is an overbearing oedipal nightmare who calls your boyfriend "my little man" and "accidentally" wanders into your bedroom when visiting due to her "poor night vision." His dad is an obsessively materialistic financial something-or-other who stops insulting your boyfriend's English degree only long enough to swill another whiskey and wink creepily. His sister believes fervently that she and her "saved" friends will be raptured to heaven in the end, and that your boyfriend is now damned to hell because you are a "heathen." These people are pretty much the exact combination of everything that annoys you, under one roof. Yet this guy is the guy you want to make your future home with. What to do?

What Doesn't Kill You . . .

The truth is, families are people we randomly are forced to spend our lives with through genetic accident. Sometimes we come to love them because we want to, but mostly, we love them because we have to. You didn't choose these people, but neither did your boyfriend. And what didn't kill him obviously made him stronger.

Just think—his mom's clinginess and lack of boundaries led him to be a strong, independent person who always knocks before he enters a room. His dad's alcoholic greed mongering led him to be a principled, generous guy who drinks moderately and winks only when his contact lenses are irritated. And his sister's fire-and-brimstone routine has helped him develop logic, religious tolerance, and a prosperous End of Days pet-sitting service.

You might not relate to these people, but they've unintentionally helped shape this guy into the man you love. Remember that, and thank them for it.

Say the Opposite

One great rule of thumb for how to talk about his family is to take whatever you actually think, run it through a special "family filter" in your head, and let it come out as something nice. So instead of saying "Your mom is bizarrely obsessed with you and thinks you're her husband," say, "I love the way your mom adores you and enjoys your company." Instead of saying, "Your dad is an alcoholic, soulless materialist," say, "Your dad clearly enjoys his career success." Just always say the opposite of what you think or a positive sounding version of the horrible thing you think. And unless they do something horrible to you, do not speak your true thoughts to your man. This will not help your cause at all. Talk to your girlfriends, to your sister, anyone but him.

If You Can't Beat 'em, Join 'em

In the beginning, getting used to another family's dysfunction is a bit of a shock. You've had your whole life to absorb and become accustomed to your own weird family. Remember, you didn't choose your folks, so why worry about whether these are the in-laws you would have chosen? You chose him, and that's the choice that matters. And just think, eventually—maybe over a lifetime—you will become so used to them that you love them like your own family. Which is to say, you find them annoying, frustrating, and difficult, but they've wormed their way into your heart anyway.

If nothing else, think about the family you want to start with him someday (although, at six months, that is *not* cool to talk about!). That's a family you will choose. And oh, boy, when Grandma and Grandpa come to visit . . .

Liking Video Games When You're with an Avid Gamer

So you've gone out a few times with a really cute, smart and funny guy you met at work. You've reached the point where you've become completely infatuated with this guy—and he seems to be really into you, too. Then one night, when the two of you go back to his apartment, you're thinking things are going to get cozy on the couch. But instead, he breaks out his Xbox 360 and starts playing *Modern Warfare 3* and *Resident Evil*. You're trying to talk to him about how much fun you had at dinner, or the latest project you're working on at the office, but he's busy collecting dog tags from defeated corpses and turning enemy soldiers into zombies. And suddenly, it hits you—unless you pretend to like video games, you're not going to get through to this guy. Speaking his language means knowing the difference between *Operation Raccoon City* and *Killzone 3*.

It's unfortunate that this awesome guy has to be so obsessed with a virtual world of blood splatter, but you're thinking he might be worth it. Therefore, you are going to have to fake liking video games! Good luck!

Turn Your Anger Into Violence

One great way to jump-start your interest in video games is to sit around some evening as your guy kills flesh-eating ghouls with a bowling ball. As you sit there, watching his entranced face staring at the wonderful carnage he has achieved, you notice he barely even knows you are there. You've been trying to talk to him about your feelings, and discuss your day, and he simply says "right" and makes something explode. After a few nights of this, you will begin to feel intense frustration.

At this time, you might be ready to start playing a video game yourself. Be sure to choose a game that is extremely violent, wherein you shoot, beat, stab, or otherwise destroy living creatures. Then pretend these creatures are guys who do not listen to their girlfriends when they talk. Imagining that these opponents are your man, proceed to beat the crap out of them and blow them to kingdom come. Your man will probably be impressed with your level of skill and energy.

Wear Cute, Game-Themed Hoodies and Shirts

Again, a good way for a girl to break through to the foreign world of boy games is to segue by way of fashion. There are a lot of super cool looking hoodies and T-shirts for many of the games that are out there. You can find that there will almost certainly be something that suits your style. It can be cool, violent, anime-looking, or goth. You can go for something tough, military and G. I. Jane, or something more soulful and tortured—depending on whether you're more angry or depressed. This can be a great way for you to express yourself, and your guy will be impressed and proud that you are "in the know." One problem could be if you are confronted or questioned about your favorite characters in these games. See my next suggestion.

Read Gaming Mags

As if being completely immersed in video games weren't enough, you can find many gaming fan magazines available, both in print and online. These will explain to you the difference between an Intelligent Partner, a live player, and deniable operations. These are very geeky little publications, featuring news, reviews, blogs, and more. You can even sample some of the games at the online version of these magazines.

This will keep you up to date and aware of some of the best games, the most popular characters, and the most recent versions of the games. It's also fun to read user forums on these gaming sites, so that you can repeat real people's comments like they are your own. You can lament how *Dead Island* has "bad aiming" and how "the zombies are all the same." It will give you guys so much to talk about! If you ever need to talk again, that is!

Knowledge about Cars

Men and cars: it's a love affair that's been going on since Fred Flintstone powered up his prehistoric vehicle with his own feet. For guys, cars have gotten all mixed up with masculinity, sexuality, power, and freedom. Men give their cars names, they talk to them, and they make weird metaphors about their engines purring. It's a creepy little bond between man and machine, one that we women can't fully relate to.

In fact, as is the case with sports teams and video games, cars are, potentially, your competitors. So you need to pretend to be cool with your rival—more than cool, even—so you don't get left in the exhaust fumes.

Having knowledge of actual cars is really not as important as having knowledge of what makes cars so alluring to guys. You want to take those qualities and emulate them. Because the last thing you want is for the "new car smell" of your man's Lexus to last longer than the "new girlfriend smell" of your relationship. Because those pine air fresheners make pretty lousy necklaces—trust me.

Gorgeous, a Little Bit Wild, but "Tamable"

Guys love the idea of a car that is equal parts flashy, classy, and wild—a car that brings out his primal self, yet also his refined qualities and his appreciation for beauty. In fact, I heard a rumor that in Prince's song, "Little Red Corvette," the "car" was actually a woman! Imagine that!

Another aspect of cars that guys love is being "in control" or "in the driver's seat." Don't worry—you don't have to actually let him be in this metaphorical driver's seat, just let him think he is. It's astonishingly easy to subtly plant ideas in a man's head and let him think they are his. Even if you let him have this feeling only once in a while, it will feel just like the best car commercial he ever saw, and he will love it.

Be His GPS

In case you think all of this testosterone-fueled car stuff seems sexist, let me point out an interesting little factoid. According to Bruce Feiler, writing for *www.nytimes.com*, most of the voices on GPS devices are female. This isn't necessarily because the voices are more helpful in providing the data, but because they're nicer. People like female voices better when being told when to turn or when to exit. So, even if your guy wants to feel "in charge" behind the wheel, don't forget that most likely, it's still a woman bossing him around. What does this mean for you? Don't be afraid to figuratively play the role of GPS woman (also known as the "navigatrix") in your relationship. Sometimes he just needs to be told which way to turn!

Let's Change a Tire!

Because I suppose I do need to share some basic information about actual cars and their boring, boring parts, I'll give you the best bang for your buck and explain how to change a tire.

According to *http://cnn.com/living*, here's how you do it. First put your car in park, and set the parking brake. Then use your owner's manual to locate your spare, jack, and tire iron. Using the tire iron, loosen the lug nuts that hold the wheel to the wheel hub. Place the tire iron on the nut, put your foot on the iron, and use your body weight to loosen the nut. Remember, righty-tighty, lefty-loosey. Jack up your car using the tire iron as a crank in the jack. Keep cranking until the car is high enough so that the tire you want to change is completely off the ground. Use the tire iron to loosen the lug nuts the rest of the way. Pull the damaged tire off. Take the new tire and line up the holes on the wheel rim with the wheel hub bolts. Tighten the lug nuts as much as possible, then lower the car slowly. Finish tightening the lug nuts, working diagonally. Remember, a spare tire is just a stopgap meant to get your car to a mechanic or tire store. Wow, you're triple A—Autonomous, Aware, and Awesome!

Being Asleep When You're Just Not Feeling Frisky

Ah, guys! Once we've weeded out the ones whose personalities force us to fake being awake, we find a good one, make a commitment, and begin a life of pretending to be asleep. Take that for irony, Alanis. It's not at all like rain on your wedding day.

In a perfect world, the old sleep fake isn't something you should need to do very often. However, you don't live in a perfect world—you live in a world where your boss's tantrums are eerily similar to your three-year-old's (although hopefully, your three-year-old's tantrums don't culminate in an epic grain-alcohol bender), your mother-in-law has insisted on making you bedazzled pajamas that say "Married to a Mama's Boy," and your to-do list might be longer than the Bible. You are so stressed out, you just now realized that those "stress balls" weren't meant to be compulsively eaten. (OMG, they are so addictive. Take them away!) All of this leaves you with the sex drive of an amoeba, but then here comes your man, looking for some single-cell action in the night. Quick, put on those bedazzled PJs and close your eyes.

Don't Snore!

One of the fastest ways to expose yourself for the lame sleep faker you are is to attempt to fake snore. Fake snoring usually only works if: (a) Your partner is heartbreakingly gullible, (b) you are amazingly convincing, or (c) you are both Looney Tunes characters. If none of these apply to you, it's best not to even try for the snore. Most people can't help but exaggerate their fake snores, giving them a theatrical, over-the-top chainsaw quality most often seen in horror flicks or mass deforestation. It's especially unconvincing if you don't even snore in the first place! So skip the snore—there's no point in making life harder than it already is. Just mouth-breathe deeply (more on this later) and count opossum—that's the animal you should count to summon pretend sleep. Yeah, I just made that up.

Drool in the Dark

Okay, so it's definitely gross, but most people do drool while they're asleep. This is because during sleep, we tend to breathe through our mouths, and we have less control over our facial muscles in general. So to add a little extra authenticity, you might want to drool just a bit while faking sleep. This is not too difficult to do; just breathe through your mouth and it should happen naturally. Or think of a shirtless Hugh Jackman. Do *not* spit—not unless you're very sure of your aim. Otherwise, what was meant to be a gentle sparing of his feelings could end up being the most insulting "no, thanks" he's ever received. (Note: Drooling can potentially backfire, if your guy thinks you are drooling over him. Use this approach carefully.)

Ideally, though, your drool won't be too much of an issue, because you will be doing your fakery in the inky void of total darkness. Everything is easier to fake in the dark! In fact, I would say that all of the advice offered in this book should, if possible, be carried out in pitch darkness or with a light-obscuring hood over the other person's head. No one will think that's weird at all!

Sleepwalk

It is possible that despite your efforts to seem asleep, your guy is just so crazy about you that he's going to keep trying no matter what. In this case, you can try to evade him by sleepwalking. Get out of bed, making sure to keep your eyes open, but stare blankly like a zombie. Grunt or babble incoherently as you plod around the house. Do this until he gives up and falls asleep (listen for the snore!). If he follows you, you can try sleep running, but I'm not sure that's a real thing. Definitely, sleep-getting-into-your-car-and-driving-to-a-hotel-so-you-can-get-some-peace is not an actual thing, so don't expect him to buy that.

A Fantastic Online Dating Profile

If there is one thing you cannot stand, it's long walks on the beach. Not only are they too freaking long, but the sand gets in your hair, you run the risk of cutting your feet on shells, and the water's freezing! And on top of all that, they make you a total cliché on your online dating profile. Frankly, you'd rather take a long walk off a short pier (Note to self: They really need to start making longer piers for distance walkers).

Look, you're complicated and interesting—hardly cookie cutter (although you do love cookie dough). So when it's time to create your online dating profile, you want to include stuff that will reflect your uniqueness and spark. However, you don't want to cross the line—too many of those "Look at me!" profiles get a flurry of short-term attention, a few dates, and then nothing. You want to be noticed in a good way, in a way that will last—because you can't build a life, a home, and a family on "winks."

Of course, if you're just looking for a bit of fun for now, by all means pull out all the stops. In the ADD-riddled world of the Internet, there is nothing easier to get than some fleeting attention. Enjoy the winks!

Be Specific

When it comes to describing yourself in an online dating profile, the opposite of "boring" is "specific." What do you think when you read in someone's profile that they "like music," "enjoy the outdoors," and "love to laugh"? Do you think anything at all in the midst of the temporary coma you've slipped into? I know I don't! I have never met a human being who doesn't at least occasionally love music, laughter, and the outdoors. These descriptors, therefore, say next to nothing about you, and are as good as wasted. I think I might be more intrigued by a person who *hates* music and laugher. At least this would make the person unforgettable in a bad way. I wouldn't want to date him, but I'd remember him. I'd tell my friends, "Remember that guy who hated music and laughter?" And we'd all laugh, which would be even funnier because that would be something that guy would totally hate.

It really doesn't take that much more effort to narrow your focus to something more specific. You could say, "Likes Inuit throat singing music," or "Loves to laugh when other people trip and fall," or "Enjoys outdoor urination." Even if what you say isn't exactly the most alluring thing ever, it's definitely going to be better than a generic catchall. Review your profile, and wherever you catch yourself generalizing, kick it up a notch. If you find yourself saying things like "enjoys new experiences," "values loyalty," or "loves life," ask yourself one question. Is there anyone on the planet who *doesn't* like the thing you're describing? If the answer is no, you're probably speaking in clichés. You can do better than that!

Picture Perfect

Okay, one thing we know is that when it comes to seeking out a mate, whether for life or for the night, looks do matter. According to *www.well cultured.com*, most singles who browse dating sites ignore profiles that lack photos. So you definitely do want to include at least one or two good, flattering photos of yourself with your profile. By "flattering" I don't mean "deceptive." The picture should be relatively recent, and be a realistic depiction of what you look like. For example, if you've shaved your head or gained 100 pounds, it's not wise to post a picture from before those changes occurred.

On the matter of flirty pictures or "MySpace–angled" pics—some websites advise against using these pictures. However, according to research from the folks at *http://blog.okcupid.com*, women who post seductive pics or MySpace-angled pics tend to do very well on dating sites. Personally, I think this kind of "success" tends to be temporary. But what do I know? Maybe your future wedding album will consist of you and your husband staring up at your cell phones as you pout seductively into a mirror. Talk about soulmates!

Liking Healthy Food

You're dating a new guy you really like and have reached the crucial stage of trying to figure out what's wrong with him. Is this guy secretly a neo-Nazi, is he the head of a large polygamous family, or does he enjoy dressing up in women's clothing? You've been nervously waiting for the other shoe to drop, and hoping it is not a Jimmy Choo strappy sandal in size fourteen wide.

Finally, you discover his fatal flaw, and it turns out even this flaw is actually a good thing—the guy is an obsessive health food junkie.

This might be good for most people, but for you, who usually has Cheez Curl dust on your fingers and considers "corn syrup" to be a food group, this is some seriously bad news. All your life, you've had a taste for nutritionally empty food items—the saltier, fattier, and more synthetic, the better. You adore sugary soft drinks, butter-loaded popcorn, and artery-clogging bacon, preferably chocolate covered. You attend state fairs just for the deep-fried Oreos. And through some thoroughly unfair stroke of genetic luck, you have managed to get away with your horrific diet. You've had no complaints. Then one day, Mr. New Guy offers to cook for you at his house—a sweet gesture and a good sign for the relationship. Except he serves you lightly sautéed vegetables, brown rice, and *tofu*. Tofu! The "curd word!"

Keep a Stash at Work

Okay, so you obviously are not going to be able to enjoy your favorite greasy, sugary delights at your man's house. Although you could keep a nasty little stash of Funyuns, cookie dough cupcakes and Happy Meals at your own house, it is possible that he may also want to visit your home, right? And you want him to! So, unfortunately, your only "neutral zone" is going to be at work, where you will want to store an extensive junk food stash in your desk. This may cause your coworkers to suspect that you are pregnant, but that's not your problem right now. Your problem is being able to hold on to that gorgeous man while still being able to pump your arteries full of Cheez Whiz, MSG, and sugar on a daily basis. If you gorge on fatty, horrible food all day at work, it will not only enable you to go to his house for an angelic dinner of organic couscous salad, but it will make your job that much more enjoyable. If, by some chance, you also work with this guy, I am so sorry. You are either going to have to break up with him or start eating healthy food. The choice is yours, but—you know—men come and go, but Nacho Cheese Combos are forever.

The Timing Is Great

Listen here, Miss Skinny Minny—you might be getting away with dietary murder now, but you're not getting any younger. The fact is, the older you get, the more your hyperactive little metabolism will slow down, and the more your body will be vulnerable to various types of breakdown. If you continue to treat yourself so horribly (even though deep fried Reese's Peanut Butter Cups feel like the best treatment ever) your body is going to punish you. That's almost a guarantee.

Luckily for you, the timing on your little ruse is just perfect. In the early stages of your relationship, you can go ahead and pig out in secret while you act all kale-loving to his face (if you get caught, claim you have a side job as a professional eater).

But by the time things get serious enough to lead to cohabitation or marriage, you will probably be reaching an age where it's smart to drop foods that spell "cheese" with a "z" anyway. So, yes, I'm telling you to fake it for a while but then *actually improve your diet.* You are lucky—this guy came along and is going to not only steal your heart but rescue its various valves and arteries. He's practically a giant defibrillator—keep him around, if only as your personal chef!

Not Ever Using the Bathroom

You have met an amazing guy, quite possibly the Love of Your Life, and you've been spending practically all of your waking hours together. It's a beautiful nonstop montage of long kisses, whispered plans of your future in the middle of the night, cuddling, and romantic dinners out on the town. He treats you like a delicate, beautiful flower, and he stares at you with wonder that such a rare, magical creature as you could exist. No one has ever made you feel so beautiful and so feminine.

So it would be really bad, after one of those romantic dinners at your favorite Mexican restaurant, for you to dump the foul contents of your intestines in his bathroom. Very un-flowerlike, even if you open a window and light a match.

The sad fact is, in the beginning of a relationship, guys in love tend to put a woman on a ridiculous, exalted pedestal, and this pedestal does *not* happen to include a toilet. Guys don't like to think women sweat, or belch, or use the lower halves of their bodies for anything but monogamous sex with them and walking.

Maybe you've found an extraordinarily amazing guy who doesn't care one bit about whether you create unpleasant aromas in his bathroom. But otherwise, all of that unsavory body business will have to wait until it's too late for him to get away. You might want to put a halt to all the Mexican food until then!

Use Public Restrooms

One excellent trick is to make frequent use of public restrooms during this pedestal phase of your relationship. When you're out on dates—which you frequently will be because he's trying to win you over—slip away into the restroom to take care of your business. One great advantage for us women is that in most cases, it doesn't take as long for us to perform this task as it does for guys. Get it done and over with quickly and shamelessly. Because you're using a ladies' restroom, there will be no chance of him catching you. Sadly, this means inflicting your nasty business on other women, which is all too often a casualty of dating. Just offer a sheepish expression and a shrug to any woman you see, and she will understand. She's probably there doing the same thing.

Potty Train Your Cat

This one will possibly take some time to achieve, but in return, it'll provide you with years and years of bathroom subterfuge. If you have a cat—and you know you do—you can teach your cat to use the toilet.

There are tons of purchasable training methods that enable you to teach your cat to effectively use the bathroom receptacles. And if your man is staying with you in your house, you can *blame your cat* for the smell in the bathroom. Simply say, "Oh, Mittens, boy did you ever make a doozy this time!" shortly after you've exited the bathroom. This strategy has the distinct advantage that you can continue to use it after the two of you move in together or get married. Just make sure Mittens comes with you. Remember, though, cats don't live forever—so you might want to work on having kids as soon as possible. Then you can blame them!

Wait a Long Time

If you are in a situation where you are forced to use a shared bathroom where your man could walk in, you should wait as long as it takes for the smell to clear the air. You might be waiting a while. According to *www.wikihow.com,*one great way to pass this time is to say you have to take a shower. I advise going to the bathroom first, then taking the shower. It's possible that the time, combined with the smell of shampoo and soap, will help reverse your odor.

If engaging in a "waiting game" challenge with your own waste isn't your idea of time well spent, there are also products out there that claim to stop bathroom odors before they even start. According to the folks at *www.incrediblethings.com*, these products are charmingly named "Poo-Pourri" and "Trap-A-Crap," and are designed to be spritzed into the commode *before* you do the deuce. The secret apparently lies in the essential oils, which create a "barrier" on the water's surface to prevent odors from escaping. Poo-Pourri and Trap-A-Crap are packaged in an assortment of delightful fragrances, including grapefruit, lemongrass and blood orange. Personally, I would have opted against the use of the word "blood" in any context involving bowel movements, but I guess that's why I am not a successful poop de-scenting mogul.

Another fine approach recommended by the writers at *www.wikihow .com* is to use the bathroom right after he's used it. Then his smell masks your smell, and he's also less likely to go right back in there again. If he does, you can always blame him. That's what love is all about!

Not Wanting to Get Married

So, you've been dating someone new, and you suspect that this guy is not overly enthusiastic about the idea of getting married. If you're not sure whether the guy you're dating is marriage-phobic, here are some signs: (a) He is a man, (b) he has male genitalia, (c) he checks off "M" on his official documents, and (d) women are the gender he prefers to date and avoid marrying.

If none of these apply to your guy, congratulations! You're either dating a woman or an awesome gay man who has recently acquired the legislative right to marry. He won't want to marry *you,* of course, but the two of you can have some great times planning *his* wedding!

If, however, you are dating the typical Joe Schmo Hetero, you can reasonably assume he fears marriage. Getting a guy to get married is sort of like taking a child to the pediatrician—they don't know it's for their own good. You have to trick them with promises of ice cream and puppet shows, and then, when they figure it out and throw a tantrum, you must gently but firmly escort them the rest of the way. Kids feel so much better once it's all over, and they get to have a free lollipop! Likewise, guys feel so much better once they've been spared the embarrassment of perpetual bachelorhood, middle-aged club hopping, and the burden of unstructured blocks of free time. See, that wasn't so bad!

Don't Protest Too Much!

You might think that the easiest, most efficient way to give a guy the impression that you don't want to get married is by simply saying, "I don't want to get married." Fine, if you're looking to win the Miss Obvious pageant, go for it. But keep in mind that there are a zillion other little ways we women unknowingly telegraph our marriage agendas without words. For this reason, these words won't be enough—even if you repeat them a million times. Maybe *especially if* you repeat them a million times. If the rest of your behavior isn't in line with your big declaration of casual noncommitment, then it's going to be about as believable as a story of an alien abduction. Besides, people who are casual about their relationships tend not to make big declarations of any kind—they just "go with the flow." When cornered, they'll say something stupid and meaningless like "it is what it is." In fact, practice saying that in the mirror—if you can manage it with a straight face, I think you'll be just fine.

No Rom-Coms!

Many of the choices you make in terms of culture and entertainment also reflect your views on marriage. You can claim to be a noncommittal free spirit until you're blue in the face, but if the only movies you want to see involve wedding planners, wedding singers, wedding cakes, wedding dresses, wedding gifts, bridal parties, and Katherine Heigl, you might just be giving yourself away. Instead, try to put yourself in the (not white satin) shoes of someone who fears and dislikes marriage. What would such a person want to see? Hint: more Godzilla, less Bridezilla. The cinematic tastes of a marriage hater would probably involve explosions, gunfights, mobsters, monsters or aliens. Or maybe it would be porn. Enjoy!

Lifestyle Tips

You should also be careful of your hobbies, interests, and figures of speech. You should avoid cooing at babies, stop attempting to reset your watch to the Biological Clock Time Zone, and don't try to get a "wedlock" installed on your front door.

Likewise, you should avoid unfortunate verbal slips. On a first date, try not to say that your meal is a "delightful marriage" of sweet and savory flavors, or that you were "engaged" by his conversation. Do not suggest that he "give you a ring" sometime. And under no circumstances should you use the word "committed," even in another context. Trust me, it won't help for you to clarify, "I meant I was 'committed' to a mental institution for stalking this guy who wouldn't marry me."

Liking Camping Trips When Your Partner Asks You to Go on One

So, you've landed yourself an outdoorsy type. Good for you! Often, outdoorsy guys are resourceful, rugged, and generally in awesome physical shape (unless by "outdoorsy,' you mean "homeless"). He seems really cool and interesting, and he appears to be into you as well. Now he's trying to take things to the next level—he's invited you on a camping trip! It will be a beautiful weekend of communing with nature and getting back to the basics of life. He's basically beckoned you into his inner sanctum.

The problem? There are few things that sound less attractive to you than sleeping on the ground in direct proximity to snakes, bugs, and snake and bug poop, having zero privacy to apply your magical makeup illusion of "natural" beauty, and having no smart phone reception. Basically, you are about as hearty as a piece of tissue paper in a tsunami, and you much prefer *campy* to *camping*. The last time a guy told you he was "pitching a tent," he was talking dirty, and your idea of "roughing it" is waking up without a Grande Cinnamon Dolce Frappuccino.

But go along with it just this once—you might win him over forever. Hopefully, on future trips, he'll opt for guys' weekends with his best pal, since you'll be his wife. Except it won't be nearly as similar to the plot of *Brokeback Mountain* as I just made it sound.

Gear Up

As I may have mentioned at various points, the best way for a girl to get excited about any hobby is to go shopping for cute outfits and accessories to go with it. You're lucky, in that camping happens to be a hobby with a full wardrobe attached to it. Imagine if your guy was into backgammon or something!

This will be fun—an excuse to buy a bunch of stuff. Go to your nearest camping or sporting goods store, and stock up on hiking boots, a parka, socks, a sleeping bag, vests, and a cute backpack. Urban Outfitters even sells a "compass necklace" that is both useful and adorable. You should also bring some "natural look" makeup that can be applied quickly and easily. Plan to wake up a little bit before he does—I recommend a watch with a beep alarm—so that you can put this on in secret. That way you will look fresh-faced and lovely, almost as if you were born that way!

Light His Fire

If you want to really impress this guy, you can offer to start a campfire for him. There are a few quick and easy cheats for achieving this. Duraflame and other fire log companies sell outdoor crackling logs, which you can combine with some real tinder to create a fast fire. Writers at *www.ehow.com* recommend putting the duraflame log on the bottom, lighting it on both ends, and placing the real logs on top of it.

Other camping supply companies sell parabolic mirrors to start a quick fire. For this to work, you have to have full sunlight so that the mirror can reflect the sun to create fire. Follow the directions that come with the product and make sure the mirror you buy is designed for camping. You don't want to just be staring at your own pretty face all night—although that's a great way to make sure your makeup is right. Once you have that fire lit, the two of you can cozy up in your sleeping bags—or better yet, in the same sleeping bag!

Liking Your Partner's Circle of Friends

You love your man, but oh, good God almighty—his *friends*. They are the type who test out electronic dog collars on themselves for fun, Photoshop your head onto the Playboy of the Month's body, and take it as an insult when you call them *Homo sapiens*. They wear so much cologne that it might officially qualify as anesthesia, and the last piece of "literature" they read was the closed captioning on the bar's TV.

Basically, your man's only friends who aren't half bald, paunchy, thirty-something kindergarteners are his *ex-girlfriends*. And while Ashley, Jenn, and Krista are much less likely to show up at your house and pull each other's fingers, they're more likely to give you backhanded compliments (I think you look *fabulous* with some extra weight), while reminiscing about the "good old days" with your guy. It's a good thing their skinny little shoulder blades are way too sharp for him to cry on comfortably, because every time you get in a fight, the Bony Blade Brigade is right there, offering him its puny consolation.

If it were up to you, you'd lose all of this deadwood and pick out some nice new friends for your guy. But it isn't up to you, and the two of you just signed on for Better or Worse. What to do?

Give Him Lots of Space

One way to convincingly like being able to stand your guy's friends is to encourage him to spend lots of "alone time" with them. Tell him you understand that he needs time with his friends—so do you. So offer the occasional "friend night," where he goes out with his buddies and you and your girlfriends get all dolled up and go out for a night on the town. Maybe one of your friends will want to post Facebook pictures of the bunch of you looking gorgeous and having fun on your own. These pictures will, no doubt, be followed by "likes" or comments like "Hot mamas!" from assorted males, perhaps even your partner's knuckle-dragging friends. Note: You *cannot* take this too far; don't go around acting flirty with other guys. Just remind him that you are totally not threatened by his friends and have an exciting, thumbs-up worthy life of your own. This will make him want to take a night off from the cavemen and put some effort into deserving the prize he's won.

Win Over the Exes

If your man is still friendly with his exes, the very worst thing you can do is act threatened by them. Being upset by their continued presence in his life shows that you are insecure and might seem like a lack of trust. Even if you don't trust them, you need to be able to trust him, or else, what's the point?

You need to not only accept them, but embrace them. No, I don't mean make out with them during the football halftime show—I mean become friends with them. This might be difficult at first, but keep at it. What you need to do is treat them like any other friend of his, except better, because they're women and you can connect over girl stuff. Compliment a new hairstyle or outfit. Say, "I really love the thin swath of material that you identify as a dress," or "That's a really cute 'I Still Love My Ex' T-shirt." Eventually, they will warm up to you and see that you really don't view them as a rival—because you know they're never going to get him back. And if they get sad, tell them you have a perfectly soft, well-nourished shoulder for them to cry on! Aw!

Liking Your Man's Sense of Style

You don't need a designer savvy, trend enslaved hipster for a boyfriend, but it would be nice if your guy could wear a shirt without stains or Sponge

Bob on it, and pants that do not include a drawstring. (Exception: If your man is a respected pediatric surgeon, and he's wearing cartoon character medical scrubs to put the sick little children at ease, I want you to drop this book and pinch yourself over your dreamlike good luck. Then punch yourself, just for good measure, and don't let me hear you whine about that man's wardrobe ever again.)

If, however, your guy is the standard issue, T-shirt and jeans-wearing slob, or if he dresses like it's the '80s—but not in a good way, or if he engages in the practice known as "sagging" (wearing his jeans so low that his underwear are fully visible), you are probably right to be somewhat mortified. We've all dated that guy whose wardrobe makes us want to crawl into a hole and die. Some of us even marry him. The reason this is such a common problem is that men, generally speaking, are clueless about fashion. Our dating options, therefore, are reduced to men whose personal style makes us cringe or guys whose meticulous metrosexuality makes us suspicious. Pick your poison, ladies, and learn to love it (or pretend to love it)—because there's only so much you can do to change it.

Don't Say It!

The one thing you should not do, especially early on in a relationship, is to tell your man that his sense of fashion is horrific. Part of loving a person is accepting some of their imperfections, and if his wardrobe is the worst thing about him, you're probably very lucky. You certainly wouldn't want him pointing out your flaws, would you? Maybe later in the relationship—like when you're both eighty—you can tell him he dresses terribly. By then, you'll probably dress terribly, too.

There are times, however, when it's okay to tell him about appropriate attire for a certain occasion. For example, you can say, "My company's holiday party is formal dress," so that he won't show up in baggy jeans and an "I'm with Stupid" T-shirt—just like he'd have the right to tell you not to wear clear plastic stripper heels to his company party. Matters of appropriateness are fine to address directly—matters of taste are not.

Help Him Out

A smarter approach to your man's woeful wardrobe is to gently and subtly make improvements. According to Los Angeles–based personal shopper Eleanor Estes, in an article on *www.cnn.com/living*, a lot of guys are the types who have literally been waiting around for a woman like you to come along and dress them. These "malleable" types are very open to fashion transformations by your stylish self. Still, though, you don't want to come out and *say* that you're making him over. Instead, take an awful item—a T-shirt, for example—and find a more stylish upgrade for him. Meanwhile, you can "lose" the old item in the bottom of the laundry hamper. Just about every type of clothing has a more stylish equivalent—except Christmas sweaters. (If your guy has those, you might just have to get him to convert to a new religion.)

Reward Improvements

Judy McGuire, author of the *www.cnn.com/living* article, suggests training your guy to dress better in the same way scientists train lab rats—through positive reinforcement. When he looks especially suave and fashionable in something you bought him, tell him how handsome he looks. Shower him with praise. Go wild with affection. Give him rat pellets—whatever it takes to get him to make the correlation that "good outfit equals happy." And in fact, you probably will naturally be even more attracted to him if he's dressed like your favorite male model. So rather than insulting his iffy fashion choices, overwhelm him with love when he dresses well. Before you know it, you'll have him trained to run through a maze for some cheese—i.e., to make an occasional trip to the grocery store!

Being Younger Than You Are to Fit Your Date's Age Preference

So, you've met a guy online who seems intelligent, interesting, and—based on his photo, anyway—*very* attractive. The two of you have exchanged a few witty e-mails and are planning to meet up for a date. The only problem? In his profile, he's stated an age preference—and let's just say you exceed that number by a few years. A few *dog years*.

Yes, you stretched the truth a bit on your profile, but you know you look younger than your age—and you feel younger, too. And if there's chemistry between you, why should you have to rule him out based on an arbitrary number?

Why? Because he said so. He chose the number; he has specified that he likes 'em young. He's written you off as "too old"—even though he's older than you! Hypocrite!

Go ahead and get mad at him in advance—you might as well. Because there's a chance he's one of those guys who can't date women his own age. He might need an adoring, wide-eyed ingénue to worship him like a god and never challenge him. Not that I am in any way familiar with, or bitterly angry about, this scenario!

Of course, he could be a perfectly decent guy who just randomly checked off an age bracket in a hurry. You may as well meet him and find out what's what.

Use Your Illusions

Normally, for first dates, it's recommended that you meet for lunch, it being an innocuous meal with minimal sexual undertones. However, if you're trying to turn back the clock, the last thing you want is a blazing midday sun shining through the restaurant windows onto your skin. So, you should suggest dinner and recommend a venue you know to be dimly lit. The dinner date may leave you fending off his advances because he's expecting to get lucky, but oh well. He can handle it. Just tell him you're tired and need to go home.

For this date, I would recommend that you apply your makeup meticulously (see: "Flawless Skin for a First Date"). There is one exception: If you happen to have adult acne that makes you look like an adolescent train wreck, you can leave that. The key word there was "adolescent." Cover the wrinkles and leave the zits. By the end of the night, you'll have that thirty-five-year-old asking you to the prom!

Also try to avoid flaunting your hands too much. Experts say that even if your face looks exceptionally young, hands are known to give away true age. So, maybe skip the handshake and give him a peck on the cheek. Fast girl!

Act Young

This is going to mean something different depending on cultural contexts of the time, but right now, at this point in our culture, to "act young" means: text constantly, use the word "epic" as an adjective and "fail" as a noun.

For example, if you should clumsily spill your soup while you're trying to simultaneously text someone, say, "Oops! Epic soup fail." Then go back to texting. Combined with those alluring zits of yours, this behavior will be the equivalent of a seduction dance.

You should also dress like a brazen young prosti-tot. Again, I can only speak for the present moment in time, which dictates that you should wear a pastel pink romper and orange riveted lace-up booties. Ask your niece.

Finally, you should make cultural references to young actors, young bands, and movies targeted to the eighteen to twenty-five demographic. Talk a lot about *Twilight.* His eyes will glaze over, but he'll still like it because it means you're young. Familiarize yourself with what the kids talk about nowadays. Do not under any circumstances utter the phrase "the kids nowadays."

Maybe, though, you'll discover that the two of you have a lot in common, and you don't have to act like a Justin Bieber groupie to maintain his interest. In that case, relax and just be yourself—or at least your first date self!

CHAPTER FOUR

Slipping On the Power Suit

Ah, the workplace. If your office is like most offices, it's like a wacky dysfunctional family with cubicles. There's the loud-talker, the microwave popcorn burner, the Bridezilla, the Happy Hour Casanova, and the boss who speaks entirely in indecipherable corporate jargon.

It's *like* a family, but it's not a family. For one thing, you're paid to put up with these people for eight hours at a time (sadly, this compensation was never offered for living with your family). Also unlike your family, your coworkers probably don't love you no matter what . . . unless you work for your family.

Your education prepared you for some of the broader aspects of your chosen field, but not for the subtle, interpersonal weirdness that happens when people are trapped together in a building all day. For example, you probably didn't learn how to pretend to be awake during a long, boring meeting, how to avoid the advances of that creepy IT guy, or how to ignore Bridezilla's loudly vocalized wedding plans. There probably wasn't a college course on how to fake having a productive day, how to not lose your cool (or your mind) during a crisis, or how to properly lie about being sick. This stuff can't be taught in a classroom— it needs to be experienced firsthand. Some of it—like the way your boss embarrassed himself at the company picnic, or the woman who compulsively cleans every surface of her work area with Clorox several times a day—you really need to see to believe.

So think of this section as picking up where your formal education left off and telling you stuff your professors never would.

Enthusiasm for a Boring Corporate Job

You weren't sure what you were going to do with that English degree when you graduated college, but you sure as hell didn't plan on becoming a "Management Facilitation Implementation Coordinator" for a "Business Matrix Resource Strategic Compliance Corporation." (Note: If reading this job description did not put you to sleep, you might be okay without this advice.) But, hey, you've got to eat—at least that's what they always say. Although after eating lunch in that gray cubicle, you're feeling dangerously close to taking a nap on your spreadsheets.

It's Like That Guy

Here's the thing about faking enthusiasm for a soul-crushing corporate job: You've won half the battle just by showing up. A corporation is kind of like a guy who's clueless in bed—full of itself, fascinated by the sound of its own voice, and utterly selfish (although, hopefully, your workplace will last longer than thirty seconds). Just think about how easy it is to fake it with that kind of guy. That's because with his inflated sense of self-worth, he naturally *assumes* you are having the time of your life. And if you're actually not? *He doesn't really care* because you're there anyway. As long as he has his fun and you make the right noises, all is right in his world.

That's kind of how it is with a boring corporate job. They've got you, they know it, and it doesn't make much difference to them if you're living your lifelong dream or if you die a little inside each time you swipe your ID badge. But they *do* expect you to make a convincing show of *pretending*. Beyond doing the actual job efficiently, this entails projecting a certain level of faux enthusiasm.

You've Got Mail!

To make it easier on yourself, you should do as much faking as you can over e-mail. In the world of e-mail, emotions can be hidden behind emoticons. (I hate you with a seething passion, thus becomes :)). Likewise, boredom can be masked with jargon (Zzzzz becomes: With respect to key performance indicators, our team promises a fast turnaround on all deliverables!) Take full advantage of all e-mail opportunities—you're very lucky to be living in an era tailor-made for fakers. Just think of the pre-e-mail working stiffs of the past—like the employees on *Mad Men*, for example. If they needed to fake enthusiasm, they had to drink a Scotch on the rocks.

Face It—and Fake It

Sometimes, despite your truly brilliant e-mail dispatches, you will be called upon to convey enthusiasm using your actual voice and face. In such situations, you'll need to step up your game a bit. Rule number one is—smile! Don't even worry about whether your smile looks false. There are a lot of fake smiles in the world, and worrying about it will only make it more strained. As long as it involves the corners of your mouth being pulled upward in an arc formation, you're a success!

Same with your voice—don't sweat whether you sound 100 percent genuine. If when you say, "That win-win is outside the box!" you aim for "psychotically excited," your natural apathy will probably bring you down to "reasonably and nonfreakishly interested." Perfect!

These tips come with one important caveat: Don't get *too* good at faking, especially when it comes to a job you can't stand. When working your faux mojo (fauxjo for short) at a soul-crushing job, the fakery should be a quick fix, not a long-term solution. Life is short. If you are bored senseless by this job, you should start plotting an escape route. Answer some ads, network online, and go to job fairs. Even if it means going back to school and giving up some fun and some sleep, isn't that better than falling asleep at your desk every day? Think of faking as being like a prescription painkiller—you can use it for a while, but don't become a junkie. Deal?

Being Sick When It's the Perfect Beach Day

Remember when you were a kid and you used to hold that old-school thermometer up to a scorching hot light bulb in order to get a day off from school? Sure, the thermometer melted and exploded into a zillion liquid metallic pieces in your hand, but that exposure to poisonous mercury was still enough to worry your mom. Mission accomplished!

Ah, how you long for those simple days of sick trickery. Now that you're a grownup, you have responsibilities, and your boss expects you to handle them in a mature and professional way. Plus, melting a digital thermometer just leaves you with a bunch of cheap, gooey plastic.

The truth is, there is not a single person in the universe who hasn't faked being sick or at least wanted to. Faux sickness is an accepted reality and not a huge deal, but you need to handle it right. No one wants to be able to see right through a lame facade, so meet your boss halfway and try to be convincing.

Less Is More

When calling in sick, your first instinct might be to go into grotesque detail about your faux illness. While I'm sure your boss would love to hear your colorful description of how squid ink pasta looks after digestion, resist the urge. Overexplanation reeks of lying. Besides, the more details you give, the more details you'll have to remember. Keep it as general and simple as possible. If you absolutely can't bear the idea of just saying, "I'm sick today," use general categories such as "sore throat," "stomach flu," or "fever." If you can avoid it, don't say "cold." Why? See "The Cold, Hard Facts."

The Cold, Hard Facts

Sure, you know that having a bad head cold makes you a wretched, socially unacceptable creature, with a runny, hideously inflamed nose, so red it could put old Rudolph out of work. Actually, you might want to inquire into that position because if you call in at work too often for colds, you're going to be jobless. It's one of those weird things in life: Everyone knows colds suck huge, but we all pretend they're no big deal. They just don't count as a "real" sickness. Never mind the fact that a recent study found that driving with a cold is comparable to driving drunk (even without the heavily spiked cold meds). If you tell your boss that you have a horrible case of the sniffles, you are going to sound wussier than the lead singer of an emo band.

A Girl Thing

Okay, now I'm going to let you in on a little bit of an unfair double standard—and this one actually works in our favor! If you have a male boss, the all-powerful "female problems" explanation continues to be a timeless get-out-of-jail-free card. Uttering those words to a male boss will make him want to get off the phone with you as quickly as possible, throw up a little in his mouth, and not talk to you again until you stop having female problems. It's a beautiful thing. Imagine a guy calling in with male problems! The very phrase is laughable—and possibly redundant. Men *are* a male problem; the least they can do is come to work!

Avoid Being Obvious

There are some days—such as Mondays, Fridays, and the day after the Super Bowl—when a sick excuse will never be believed. I repeat: Will. Not. Be. Believed. Even if it's the truth, the whole truth, and nothing but. On days like this, you can bet yours won't be the only message on Bossy McBosserson's voice mail. People are predictable that way, and you don't want to be predictable. So unless you are truly feeling awful, try to avoid taking sick days that scream "early weekend" (Friday), "epic hangover" (Monday), or "suspiciously tan" (obscenely gorgeous day). Although if you happen to be the type who burns instead of tans, a day spent in the sun can double nicely as a fever flush. Good for you, Lobster Girl!

Confidence During an Important Presentation

You're fairly new at your job, and you've been working like a dog. (But not one of those lazy dogs that lies around snoring all day in a fancy sweater. You're an employed dog, like a sled dog or a drug-sniffing dog. But wait, you totally don't sniff drugs, either. Let's just say you're working hard).

And it's paid off! Your boss is so impressed with your diligence and hard work that she wants *you* to give an important presentation for your department to the company's entire board of directors.

Ack! Reward? You might prefer a *reward* that involves being placed on a wooden rack and being stretched in separate directions until you can hear your joints forcibly dislocating. Public speaking, unfortunately, is just not your thing.

Like it or not, though, this seems to be your big chance to get on the radar of the company bigwigs. You've been working all this time to make a name for yourself. You just don't want that name to be "Awkward McFreakout."

Prepare Yourself!

According to Josh Briggs of *http://money.howstuffworks.com*, the best way to overcome your nerves and look confident during a presentation is to be prepared. If you know your material well and have enthusiasm for it, that feeling will resonate. Practice your speech in front of a small group of friends or a mirror. Don't break the mirror—it's much better to break your leg. A fracture of your femur means your speech will turn out well, but a breakage of a $7.50 mirror from Kmart spells disaster. Plus, if you are lucky enough to break your leg, everyone will be so focused on your cast that they won't care about your presentation.

Briggs also advises imagining your presentation like a story, dividing it into beginning, middle, and end. Think of each little section like chapters. This will help you structure the presentation and organize it in your mind, so you'll be able to feel more confident even if public speaking is your greatest fear.

Use Visuals

If you are a self-conscious individual (this means *you*, you), the last thing you are going to want is to have everyone staring at you during the entire presentation. If you feel the fiery laser heat of thirty-five high-ranking pairs of eyes on you as you speak, you're likely to break under the pressure (and I don't mean your other leg, either—you should be so lucky).

A great way to divert the attention from you and put it back on the content is the use of visual media. You can use a PowerPoint presentation, charts or graphs, illustrations, or even a video if applicable. Not only will this take the heat off you, it will help keep your audience awake. The human attention span is pretty limited, so if you can give them some new, colorful stuff to look at, they'll be as mesmerized as a baby staring at those multicolored plastic keys. Remember, if you are using Power-Point slides with information on them, don't simply read that same information aloud; it's redundant. Instead, elaborate a little bit on what the slide is showing.

Focus on the Message

Another useful strategy in keeping your composure during a presentation is to remind yourself that this isn't about you. You are simply the conduit, the instrument through which this important information is being conveyed. This is something these folks need to know about, and you need to tell them. If the building were on fire and you went to tell your coworkers that smoke and flames were ravaging the cafeteria, you wouldn't think, "OMG, do I look fat in this burning skirt? Did I stutter over the words 'smoke inhalation'?" Well, maybe you would. But your first concern would be to communicate the essential facts: Fire. Building. Here.

Look, the truth is, this is about you. But that's something for you to revel in later, after you've totally nailed it. For now, just focus on the message, and make sure you get the essentials out there. So, are you out of intact leg bones at this point? Then break an arm!

An Awesome Resume When You're Not That Qualified for the Position

So, you saw a listing for a job you just *know* you'd be perfect for, and you can't wait to apply. You've envisioned your new life with this amazing job—your days would be a delirious haze of nonstop excitement, achievement, and paycheck spending. There's just one teensy problem—you're not exactly qualified for this job. At all. Really, though, when exactly were you supposed to get experience stuffing envelopes for $8,000 a month? To make matters worse, you're not even a single mom, which seems to be an important prerequisite!

Actually, for a job like that, I wouldn't worry too much about your resume. I would worry about how many envelopes you'll need to stuff into your mouth to keep the cavernous hunger at bay once you've spent all your money on a "Getting Started Envelope Kit!" and can no longer afford groceries. (You'll want to double-lick the envelopes for extra nutrition! Good thing you're *not* a single mom!)

The point is that some job ads require "no experience!" and use a lot of exclamation points (!!!) because they're scams. However, most valid jobs require that you have some experience in that particular field.

Believe it or not, you can present yourself well even if you aren't a perfect match for the job. It's just a matter of looking good on paper!

Don't Overcompensate!

At some point in this process, you might have thought to yourself, "Okay, so I'm not qualified—I'll just make up for that with lots of fancy fonts, leopard print paper, and a magazine's worth of perfume on the document. That'll do it."

As great as that sounds, I'm here to tell you that business professionals tend not to like "fun" fonts, emoticons, or colorful print jobs—at least not in a resume. You can't just make them forget that you have no experience by distracting them with pretty, shiny things, okay? That's what the *interview* is for. For the resume, simply show your seriousness and professionalism with a simple, black and white document, no cutesy stuff.

Don't Pad—Lift!

There's a difference between a padded bra and a pushup bra: A padded bra adds synthetic stuffing to your natural endowments, while a pushup bra gently lifts and accentuates what you already have. So it should be with your resume: You want a "pushup resume."

If you don't have relevant work experience, you should list any extracurricular activities or volunteer work you have done in that area. Otherwise, list all jobs and extracurricular activities where you've used the Universal Skills: dealing with humans, writing, speaking, and reading. These are skills we all use daily, and they can be applied to most any job. You might want to present your experience through what the writers at *www.wikihow.com* call a "functional resume" rather than a "chronological resume." Instead of listing your jobs in chronological order, list your most relevant experience first.

In the meantime, between jobs, it's always smart to cultivate other interests or hobbies through organized projects or clubs. You might be able to use the experiences and skills learned from participating in them on a future application.

Express Yourself Well

Communication skills are fundamental to almost any job (except maybe for weird math stuff), so it's essential that you use good grammar, punctuation, and spelling on your resume. A killer cover letter is also a great way to catch the interest of a hiring manager. If you present yourself as a dynamic, articulate person who can communicate well, you'll increase your chances at getting any job. Special note: If you are sending out multiple resumes or cover letters, *please* be sure to customize your materials for each specific job. You would be surprised at how many people send out "form resumes" and cover letters without updating them to suit the job in question. It might be easier for *you* to send out a letter telling a grade school that you'd be "great at training their animals," but it might hurt your chances of landing an interview. Oh well, envelopes for dinner again!

Keeping Your Cool When Problems Arise at the Office

You've probably had a job where some smarty-pants manager has told you that you'll need to "check your ego at the door," "check your baggage at the door," or "check your crazy obsession with the water cooler delivery guy at the door." If only! Imagine what an incredible baggage check system that would be! At the end of the day, when you see your wacko emotional issues going around the carousel, you could just leave them there.

In reality, as much as we professional people try to pretend otherwise, we all show up for work with a full set of working emotions. We can try to curb them (at least the negative ones) all we want, but they still exist.

In many ways, your most basic emotions—anger, fear, sadness, jealousy—haven't evolved much from the way they were when you were five years old. Thus, when these emotions are allowed to rule, you could potentially act like a five-year-old throwing a fit. Not good for your chances for a promotion.

So when your boss is getting on your case about something totally unfair—your coworker gets a promotion you know you deserved, or your clients are tormenting you with last minute demands in the face of a deadline—how do you keep that explosive five-year-old at bay? Believe it or not, an ice cream cone is only part of the answer. Here's the rest.

Buy Time and Breathe

According to Elizabeth Lowman, writing for *www.forbes.com*, the whole "count to ten and take a breath" thing that your mom used to do instead of spanking your ornery flanks still works. Of course, you should *not* threaten to flog colleagues at the end of ten seconds, especially if it's your boss. Instead, this should be a private thing, wherein you retreat inside to a happy place and practice yogic breathing while not saying the horrible, career-destroying thing you want to say. Will it look weird, you standing there and taking measured breaths after your coworker waits for you to reply to the verbal dump they just unloaded on you? Maybe—but it's much better to be known as "That Weird Woman Who Doesn't Say Anything for Ten Full One-Mississippi Seconds" than "That Woman Who Told the Boss That He Clearly Has a Napoleon Complex of the Penis," otherwise known as "That Woman Who No Longer Works Here." An even better way to buy time is to simply suck up your emotions, walk away, and continue the conversation over e-mail. Once you have retreated to the safe haven of the Internet, you can put your meltdown on ice and craft a composed, rational, and emotionally neutral version of your thoughts on the matter. In other words, say the exact opposite of what you feel. If, in reviewing the e-mail, you notice a sentence that speaks to your gut instincts, tweak it right away. After all, that's the beauty of the Internet: there is never any need for a kneejerk reaction, unless your knee has a ridiculously delayed jerk mechanism. If so, don't worry—there are probably drugs for that.

Find a Venting Buddy

Lowman also recommends finding a trusted work friend to vent to about your stress, anger, disappointment, and jealousy. Chances are, there is at least one person at your office who is discreet, trustworthy, and starved for gossip. You don't want to wallow or talk their ear off, but maybe a little lunchtime venting session will help you blow off some of that steam. Possibly, your friend will offer some perspective or commiseration—perhaps something along the lines of, "Oh, I've had the exact same problem with X."

Keep in mind, too, that although venting is best known for its fulfilling emotional purge, it can also lead to a useful exchange of ideas and even some great fakes. Your friend might be well versed in corporate speak and provide you with the words you need (i.e., "I've had a robust pre-think with the team, and we're vectoring toward going live with this ASAP,") to get X off your back until you actually figure this mess out.

Remember: Bad Days End

It's true that you can't leave your emotions at the door of your office when you come to work in the morning, and likewise, you can't leave them at the office when you go home. But try to remember that a bad day is just that—a bad day. You can go home, take a hot bath, eat some fudge walnut brownies, drink some wine, and go to bed. Maybe after a night's sleep, a small pity soiree, and some time away, you'll have a better perspective on how to handle the issue, or at least be able to suck up your pride and lie about your feelings for the greater good. And you'll be so happy you got through the day without kicking your boss right in the source of his troublesome testosterone! You deserve another glass of wine just for that!

Being Interested in Your Coworkers' Plans for Their Future Children or Wedding

First there was your office's resident Bridezilla, who happens to work two cubicles away from you, and whose voice can be heard shrilly arguing with wedding planners about origami swans vs. live butterflies, chicken satay vs. crab cakes, and which creepily oedipal song she should dance to with her father. You thought that was bad enough.

Then the woman who sits next to you got engaged. Now, everywhere she goes, female shrieks can be heard in reaction to the gigantic, twenty-four-karat monstrosity she's lugging around on her finger. Her new job title seems to be "Interoffice Diamond-Showing Liaison," and she's good at it. She won't rest until every single person in the building has beheld the emerald-cut hunk of radiance that symbolizes her love. You've nicknamed her Ring Kong, and you fantasize about "Ring Kong vs. Bridezilla," an epic showdown to the death fueled only by uncooked rice and Save the Date cards. Awesome.

Then, of course, there's Preggy Peggy, who is lobbying your workplace for an official "Pump Room" and who has secured a "Lactation Coach," whom you imagine holding a clipboard, wearing a tracksuit, and telling Peggy to "drop and give me twenty units of milk" during her workout in the "Pump Room."

Really, you wish these ladies well—honest! You just wish you didn't have to hear every detail of their marital and reproductive futures. Sorry, but you do. You totally do.

Pretend She's a Reality Show

You've watched reality shows about crazy wedding dramas, conflicts and pettiness, right? Well, you have one right in your office now. Sure, everything's all shiny and new at the start, but by the time these girls get to the altar, they will have been dragged through a self-imposed hell that is truly like no other. You'll get to overhear Bridezilla crying into the phone about how she "failed" her latest dress fitting or interrogating her fiancé about his strange new attachment to the gag blowup doll he got at his bachelor party. (*She* would have no trouble with the dress fitting! She can just deflate!) You can listen to Ring Kong despairing about finding a wedding ring worthy of her beautiful engagement ring or lamenting the carpal tunnel syndrome she's acquired from its bone-crushing weight. You can sympathize with Preggy Peggy over her worries that her baby will suffer from "nipple confusion." You can't make stuff like this up, and really, it is priceless. You have a three-ring circus going on in your office! How could you *not* be interested? Sit back and enjoy the show!

Discuss Current Events!

If reality TV isn't your thing, you can always meet halfway and bring the conversation around to something that does interest you, like current events. For example, you can talk to Ring Kong about her fancy ring and how Liberian warlords probably used it to wage civil unrest and commit atrocious crimes against humanity. It'll be so educational! You all can sit around and discuss how pretty diamonds like hers enabled the Revolutionary United Front to force children into becoming soldiers and killing their own parents before they even lost all their baby teeth. But it's so sparkly!

Walk in Her Shoes

Okay, if you're not into reality TV *or* current events, I'm not sure what's left. I mean, I think I've covered most network and cable TV programming.

You might just have to fall back on the golden rule: "Do unto others as you would have them do unto you." Remember, at some point, it might be you making the Big Plans. And although you are absolutely certain you would never do unto others any of the wacko nonsense these women have done unto you, try to empathize. You would want people to at least seem interested, right? It's nice to know your coworkers care about an important milestone in your life. Especially if that milestone happens to be a princess cut with fifty-eight facets and may have financed an entire insurgency in Zimbabwe!

Having a Productive Day

Maybe it's a really gorgeous day outside, or maybe you're in a huge fight with your significant other, or maybe you are incredibly tired, sick, hungover, or distracted. Or perhaps it's the simple fact that the garish wattage of the fluorescent lights, the gray, institutional carpeting, and the sickly glow of your computer screen are just not igniting your motivation like they usually do. The writing is on the wall: You're going to be useless today. You could try to fight it, but frankly, you don't want to. The best you can do is to be a warm body in a chair.

Here's the good news—if you're a warm body in a chair, you've won half the battle. Few things bring supervisors more delight than glancing around a room and seeing warm bodies installed in every chair, feverishly faux-working. It doesn't matter if your brain is about as sharp as strained baby food. If you're shuffling papers around in an important-looking way, you're playing a valuable part in maintaining the company image.

I should qualify this by saying that if you have an actual deadline to produce something today, you'll need to suck it up and do it. As far as I know, there's no way to fake actual output, unless you get someone else to do your work for you. And if you're the kind of genius who can get someone else to do your job, you don't need me!

Post It!

According to *www.lifehackery.com*, one great way to seem like you're incredibly busy at work is to plaster your computer monitor/work area with Post-it Notes. This makes it seem as though you have a great deal of important things going on and that you are very industrious about keeping track of them. Although the notes don't necessarily have to pertain to a real project, they should at least be relevant enough so that if your boss zooms in for a closer look, they make sense. Every once in a while, pull one of them off, study it for a long time, and then start typing for a while. Eventually, you can discard the note, which suggests you've finished the task described on it.

Lots of Typing

A very tried-and-true method of seeming productive is to type. A lot. Typing, especially if it is done in a brisk and secretarial manner, trumps paper shuffling in these increasingly paperless times. The sound of typing is like the pleasant white noise of an office environment, and it makes bosses happy to hear it. Even if you are typing an e-mail to your best friend about how nobody needed to make a "Smurfs" movie.

Word of caution: some bosses, occasionally, actually want to know what you're typing. They'll walk by to just casually see if they can bust you typing a Facebook status, an e-mail, or an eBay bid. For this reason, I suggest typing e-mails in a Microsoft Word document first, then stealthily pasting them into your e-mail when they're done. If your boss walks by and you're typing away in a Word document, it's doubtful he or she will look closer.

Game Camouflage

It used to be that we developed new technologies to make life more efficient. Now, we've reached a point where we're so efficient, we need technologies just to slow stuff down. Enter the Internet—the most wonderful time-suck since the invention of sleeping.

In fact, there are several websites designed to "camouflage" time-wasting computer games in a "professional" looking screen. One of the more brilliant of these, at *www.cantyouseeimbusy.com*, encrypts various video games in spreadsheet or day planner formats. The games have titles like "Leadership," "Cost Cutter," and "Crash Planning" and can even be customized with your company's name. All of this looks about as interesting as an accountant's dreams and is unlikely to raise even the slightest suspicion in a boss who happens to stop by. In fact, all the migraine-y "charts" and "graphs" will likely drive your boss away, both out of trust in your work ethic and the sudden need for a nap. Okay, back to Spreadsheet Space Invaders!

Knowing What You're Doing When Your Manager Wants You to Take On A Complicated Project

Whoever came up with the expression "There's no such thing as a stupid question" has clearly never met your boss. He's one of those guys who rattles off, in one impatient sentence, a request for you to split the atom by the end of the day, then concludes with, "You can handle that, right?" In case you didn't know, there's only one acceptable answer to that question, and it isn't, "I want my mommy."

Of course, Mr. Vague is also notoriously annoyed by follow-up questions, even ones that are perfectly reasonable. Now he's paid you the "compliment" of assigning you a very important, almost entirely incomprehensible project. He just stopped at your desk, cleared his throat, and uttered such a rapid-fire, nonsensical mash-up of corporate jargon and

SAT vocabulary words that you're not even sure what your name is anymore. Well, whatever your name is, Boss Crazyhead is trusting you with something you don't even think you can pronounce.

Ask for a Sample or Template

Since it seems that much of your boss's leadership technique relies upon the mind reading capabilities of his underlings, and you, unfortunately, don't possess those powers, read up on how other coworkers tackled the project. If this assignment involves a written report or other document, ask your boss if you can study some of the materials from previous projects of this nature—particularly ones that were done well. Just say that you want to study the materials so you can understand what sets a successful effort apart. This will make you seem ambitious and thorough, without revealing you don't know what the hell you are doing. Hopefully, if you can get your mitts on some previous samples of this type of work, they will give you clues about how it should be done. It'll be like solving a murder mystery, except you'll actually be preventing a murder—the murder of your career. Or your boss.

Talk to Someone Who's Been There

Hopefully, the project you've been assigned is something that someone else in your office has handled before (who *hasn't* split an atom at some point?). If this is the case, choose someone who seems understanding and empathetic, maybe treat them to lunch, and ask them for some pointers. Again, you don't need to volunteer the information that you're absolutely clueless, although if you're lucky, they might tell you that they once felt the same way. Make sure to be cautious about saying anything negative about the boss, though. Probably everyone knows he's a freak, but you don't want to be the person who says it out loud.

The good news is you've found someone who is willing to share his or her wisdom with you. Learn everything you can from this person, and before you know it, you will genuinely know what you're doing!

Knowing a Coworker You Never Interact With

Maybe you're at the company picnic and have been randomly paired up for the egg toss competition with someone who has never said "boo" to you—or worse, someone who *has* said "boo" to you. Or maybe you've been sent on a business trip to Dubai with a guy you don't know from Adam (at least they didn't send Adam—that guy's a real creep). Or maybe an important client asks you if you know his favorite sales associate, let's call her Person-You-Have-Never-Interacted-with-Except-the-Time-You-Burned-Popcorn-in-the-Lunchroom-and-You-Smiled-Sheepishly-at-Her-As-You-Slunk-Away-in-a-Trail-of-Smoke. Actually, that's kind of long. Let's call her Lisa.

The reality is that most offices keep people as compartmentalized in their little cubicles as zoo animals in cages. We rarely move outside our own little enclosures to interact with those exotic species in other departments.

To the outside world, though, we're supposed to seem united, a team, aware of one another's existence. So when you get thrown into an unexpected collaboration with an unfamiliar coworker, you need to act like you're on the same team. Ideally, the other person will recognize the need for this fakery and play along. If not, you may have to appoint yourself imaginary team captain and call the plays until your teammate picks up on your strategy and starts executing the fakes like an old pro. If you do it right, the two of you will hit this thing right out of the park—unless we're talking about the egg toss at the picnic. In that case, please be gentle and do not hit the egg at all.

More Sports Metaphors

If you were playing a game of soccer, you wouldn't need to know your teammate well to pass the ball for a game-winning goal, would you? No. You would just know what your roles were on the team and relate to each other that way. If you were the pitcher and your coworker were the catcher, you wouldn't need to be BFFs to understand her elaborate hand signals and weird finger wiggling, right? Hardly. If you were on the same professional wrestling team, you wouldn't have to be pals with your partner, Buff Bagwell, to let him break a chair on your head as a trick on your opponents, the Wolfpac, would you? Yes, a wooden chair. Yes, directly onto your face—what else are chairs for?

Anyway, the point of this is that you and your colleague already have a lot in common: namely, a shared mission. If you focus on your common goal, whether it's acing a presentation or not getting chair splinters in your eyes, you will bond surprisingly quickly.

Drop Names, But Don't Drop the Ball
(Unless the Person's Name Is Ball)

So, suppose you have to fake knowing a coworker without the advantage of that person being there to play along. For example, let's say you have an important new client, Alistair Shmoe, and you're meeting with him for the first time. He says, "You work at X Company, so you *must* know Blah Blah." Unfortunately, you have never met Blah Blah and know next to nothing about him. But you don't want to stare blankly at your new client, or ask him who the hell Blah Blah is. Even worse, you don't want to take a wild guess at some tidbit of information to prove you know the man. You should simply say something vague but positive about Blah Blah. You can say something like, "Blah Blah does good work. I haven't worked closely with him, but I've heard good things." Perfect. You seem in the know but not like a know-it-all. Go team!

Knowing the Answer to Your Client's Question

It's been a long day, and just as you're about to pack up and go home, you get a call from an important client. She's asking if your company would be able to supply her with 150 units of Product X and 200 units of Product Y by close of business on Friday. (They're all good on Z's, apparently. So are you, as evidenced by the contents of the cartoon thought bubble over your head.)

You are an ambitious, relatively new associate at your company, and you would love to dazzle this woman by promising her more Xs and Ys than a chromosomal hermaphrodite. However, you have no idea how long it would take your company to produce 150 of Product X, and you're not even sure what product Y is. Now what?

Well, of course, the last thing you want to sound like is exactly what you are: a new person who isn't really sure what she's doing yet. There's something off-putting about customer service that whittles down to a fancy equivalent of "duh."

But how do you fake knowing what you don't know without the thing you don't know coming back to bite you in the butt? Especially since it's something you don't know; a bite in the butt from this thing could be lethal.

Underpromise, Overdeliver

The whole underpromise/overdeliver trick is a little mind game that has worked well in business for many years. Nobody really minds that you've fibbed a bit in your underpromise, because your overdelivery is effing awesome.

It's sort of like an encore at a concert by your favorite band—the band's sort of like, "Bye, now! That was totally our last song, we swear! We are *definitely* not coming back, not even if you clap a whole lot!" When the band does come back onstage to play one last rousing rendition of "Year 3000" (ew, why are you at a Jonas Brothers concert?), you don't think, "What liars!" You think, "They surpassed my every expectation!" That's the crux of the old underpromise/overdeliver strategy.

So how this would work is you tell your client, "Nope, we definitely do not have any Xs or Ys, that's for sure. Sorry, lady, but there are no ifs, ands, or buts about our Xs and Ys." Then go find out if there really are any Xs or Ys, and if there are enough to meet her request, make it seem like you moved mountains to get them for her. The only potential problem here is if she has already moved on to another vendor for her Xs and Ys. Then your overdelivery would be more like overkill. And when it comes to kill, people usually prefer underkill or just the right amount of kill.

Admit You Don't Know

According to Janine Popick, writing for *www.inc.com*, it's not always the best idea to pretend you know the answer when you don't. There's a name for that type of person—a know-it-all.

As much as a client might huff and puff about your admitting that you don't know, they will ultimately appreciate the fact that you value their time enough to be honest. Imagine if you promised them all the Xs and Ys they could handle, and then later had to tell them it turns out your company doesn't even make Xs or Ys?

Of course, you can dress this up a bit—you don't have to come right out and say, "Um, I have absolutely no clue." Instead, maybe say something like, "Listen, I just want to check and make sure we have the resources to help you with this. I will get right back to you." Then you can call them back or e-mail them with the answer. Even if they don't love your answer this time, they will remember you as a straight shooter who takes time to do your research before you speak. It's simple professionalism. Look, people dislike know-it-alls even in kindergarten—why should that change now?

Staying Awake During a Meeting

It's 2:00 P.M., and if you were living in a much more awesome country with a more laid-back culture, you'd be taking a siesta. After a heavy midday meal, full of carbs and maybe some alcohol, you and all your colleagues would go home and sleep for two or three hours. You'd awake refreshed, alert, and much more capable of taking on the day's remaining tasks. You would arise safe in the knowledge that the two or three hours you spent in dreamland would have only been wasted fighting sleep at your desk, or—even worse—fighting sleep as you struggled through the pharmaceutical grade sleep remedy known as the midafternoon meeting, which, in case you didn't see it coming, is what you are doing right now.

It's such a cruel joke, scheduling meetings right after lunch, when full consciousness is about as attainable as a winning lottery ticket. Especially meetings pertaining to expense report reimbursements and budgetary line item additions. *Double especially* when this information is being delivered by the company's head of accounting, a man with the most droning, hypnosis-inducing voice you have ever heard in your life. And the meeting just started five minutes ago.

Paint Eyes on Your Eyelids

A classic approach to seeming awake during a meeting is to paint eyes onto your eyelids. This is a trick you'll need to do beforehand so either do it at home or slip into the ladies' room. You might want to make the faux eyes a little bit bigger than your own natural eyes, so you'll seem almost ridiculously alert. You can even get the eyes tattooed permanently on your lids! Try to maintain as straight a posture as you can while slipping off into your siesta, so that you'll seem wide-eyed, attentive, and eager to learn. Try not to snore. You should also try not to drool, since an unblinking stare and nonstop drooling might give the accounting director the mistaken idea that you have a crush on him.

Periodically Ask Questions

You probably will be jarred out of your REM sleep at a few points during this meeting anyway, so you should try to make use of your occasional wakefulness to ask a question or two. Jolting awake suddenly does draw attention to you, so when that happens, just ask a general question like, "How do we facilitate this?" or "What is the value proposition?" If just waking up makes you seem really startled when you ask these questions, all the better—you will seem very concerned, even urgently so. Asking questions or making comments during a meeting definitely makes it seem as though you are conscious and maybe even paying attention.

Think about Getting Fired

One way to try to genuinely stay awake during a meeting is to imagine getting fired over it. Picture the boss calling you into her office, closing the door in that horrible telltale way, and saying those chilling words, "This just isn't working out." Then imagine having no money for the rent and having to live with your mom, who will leave classified ad clippings on your childhood bed, make you go with her to bridge night with her old lady friends, and try to fix you up with her dentist, who has a hairy mole and smells like geriatric teeth. Imagine having to get a job dressing up as a giant slice of pizza and waving at people on the interstate. Imagine marrying the awful dentist in desperation and then never being able to feign sleep because you've had open eyes tattooed on your lids. Imagine all this, and if it doesn't wake you up, I don't know what will!

Being Helpful over the Phone

Once upon a time, there used to be a thing called telephone customer service. In these olden days, many years ago, telephones were not used to reroute, confuse, frustrate, or musically torture callers. Customer service representatives did not play the hilarious game of wearing callers down with endless robotized prompts, dial-by-name directories, and menu options that were always being "recently changed." Back then, you didn't have to give a different name every time you answered and tell the customer the exact opposite of what you'd said the last time. You actually answered the phone when it rang (it actually rang!), and you just answered the question as best as you could. You didn't record the call for quality assurance purposes, or subject the caller to long blocks of hold time while encouraging them to go online instead. Sometimes, you even *called people back*.

These days, as we all know, the only way to get that kind of personalized telephone service is to call a phone sex line. Even a torture fantasy with a telephone dominatrix is more merciful than trying to navigate the robo mind games of the typical customer service line. But since everything old eventually gets recycled as "retro," there will inevitably come the day when your boss longs for those golden days of great service. At this time you will have to actively *try* to help the other person on the line, even if only ironically. Here are some strategies for providing great customer service without feeling like you're the one being punished.

Be Human

If you are an employee who wants to fake being helpful over the phone, you are in great luck. The bar for telephone helpfulness has never been lower. Telephone "customer service" is more of an ironic mockery of itself than anything else. People who call seeking help on the phone fully expect to be disappointed and messed with. So if you can actually sound human and helpful, you will blow their little minds. For starters, try not to sound like a robot. This will be difficult at first, since you've probably been trained to do the opposite, but after a while, it will start to feel almost natural. Go out of your way to be empathetic to the caller's problem, tell them about a time you had the same problem, and maybe make a joke or two. Most of all, don't actively try to subvert them or be obviously unhelpful. You can even tell them your first and last names, and if you're allowed, your extension or direct number. Wow!

Do Something for Them

Depending on your company and its particular objectives and rules, your hands may be tied as far as helping the customer. But if you can do a little bit to resolve the callers's issues, they might just start a religion in your name. If you're acting human and being kind, they're already eating out of your hand. So see if you can actually work on helping these fellow humans out. Just imagine what it would be like for you if a customer service rep actually helped you! It would be like a very special episode of *Touched by an Angel*. That is how these people will feel if you give them what they asked for.

I would advise you to tread carefully with this "helping people" stuff— if you establish yourself as too much of an overachiever, the rest of your office might resent you. There's no need to be a "goody-goody." Or even "good." Just do the bare minimum—it will be way more than anyone has seen in years!

Understanding Your Boss's References

So, you started a new job in your chosen field, the vocation you studied extensively over the course of your four years in college. You think you know what the job requires of you, and since you were hired, you can only assume your boss feels the same. Then, during the first week of your employment, your boss and various higher-ups said many terrible and confusing things to you. Things like:

"We need to drill down to the ROI and develop a turnkey solution."

"We need a silver bullet from those thought leaders. I don't want to shoot the puppy on this one."

"Ping me about the mature onboarding. We need to use best practice methodology to incentivize our supply chain."

You *thought* you understood this job; for that matter, you *thought* you understood the English language. But after hearing your boss spout this gibberish, you're pretty sure your job is to translate from the native language of planet Uranus.

Sadly, while college often provides a solid academic foundation, it does very little to prepare us for the weird curriculum of the corporate world. Corporations like to come up with their own encoded language—which to an outsider sounds terribly confusing—to trick the world into thinking they are doing something very technical and difficult. In reality, they're probably watching YouTube videos of foxes jumping on trampolines. Regardless, though, you need to understand your boss—and he can't, or won't, speak normally.

Pick Up On Context Clues

Eventually, you will begin to decipher this language just by observing the meaning of the words in context. For example, if someone is supposed to get "pinged" and they remain uninjured by the end of the day, then it didn't involve being shot with a BB gun, as you originally thought. If someone who was given a "golden parachute" never comes back to the office again, it didn't mean they were destined to "rise to the top," like you'd assumed. And all that worry you put yourself through after your boss said your idea was "hand grenade close" was completely unnecessary. Turns out that didn't mean it was a total bomb, or in the language of *Jersey Shore*, an unattractive girl. It was actually a compliment!

Other terms can be decoded by how they sound. "Smirting," for example, is a hybrid of smoking and flirting, and, accordingly, means flirting with coworkers during a smoke break. "Sympvertising" is advertising aimed at consumers' sympathy. So just spend some time watching and listening, and eventually, you'll understand the meanings through cause and effect. Hopefully, you'll figure it out before you get the golden parachute!

Consult a Glossary

You'll be relieved to know that many people are, like you, utterly dumbfounded by many of the references made in the workplace. As a result, there are many glossaries of corporate jargon and office-speak. Some of them are books and some are websites, but all of them attempt to clarify and demystify this weird nonlanguage used in offices. For example, you'll find out what an "ear job" is, or a "brain dump," or "management porn" (thank God this does not involve your boss in an X-rated film). These resources are not only useful in cracking the code a little bit faster, but they're tremendously amusing. You definitely will want to drill down into this brain dump!

Once you do learn and master corporate jargon, the next step is to not use it. It's one thing to understand it—that will help you to get by and ping effectively. But according to Heidi LaFleche on *http://career-advice .monster.com*, corporate speak not only doesn't make a person sound smarter, it also makes them less likeable to others. So you should set yourself apart from your colleagues, and be the person who speaks clear English. Everyone will want you to give them an ear job!

Having Exciting Weekend Plans

Maybe you sit next to your office's resident socialite, who has something awesome going on every single weekend (and whose purse Chihuahua keeps shimmying into your snack drawer and eating all of your "I-live-at-the-office" treats). Or perhaps you still have to interact with that cute guy you went on a few awkward dates with before he never called you again. Or perhaps there's a not-so-cute guy who shows up at your cubicle each Thursday at noon to inquire about your weekend plans.

Whatever your motivation, you don't want to be the girl with nothing on the agenda this weekend but a *Bones* rerun marathon, the alphabetizing of your DVD collection, and the introduction of a tiny basketball hoop into your fish tank. Although these are all perfectly valid activities, they are dead giveaways that you "have a life" only in the literal sense that you have a pulse and are circulating blood. In fact, if someone were to check your pulse, insinuating that you might be undead, that would be a huge compliment. You *wish* you had the social life of a vampire!

Now, as if you weren't already giving your entire week to this job, it seems you're also required to maintain some sort of weekend "image control." You must conceal the fact that most of your weekends are about as exciting as a hand sanitizer convention. You know this because you've attended a hand sanitizer convention.

The Phone Call

One of the best strategies for broadcasting your oh-so-exciting weekend plans is to get a phone call from a friend discussing said plans. You have a few choices for how to play this one: You can either discuss your plans in a loud voice, so that everyone can hear all about them, or you can discuss them in a loud whisper, which is even better. The loud whisper will intrigue your audience, because it implies a juicy secret, but it's so flipping loud everyone will be able to hear it anyway. So, it's both attention grabbing and exhibitionistic, while also seeming "discreet." During your conversation, be sure to say lots of things that imply exciting scandal, like, "OMG! Please tell me he is *not* going show his face there! Are you kidding? Does he know she's coming too? Oh, this is going to be *awesome!*"

You can also drop little clues that suggest that you're incredibly popular, such as, "Well, hmm, maybe I will stop by that party for a while, and then meet up with you guys at the club later."

The phone call can either be a real, interactive call with a friend (or your mom, if you're really desperate) who agrees to contact you at a strategic time, or you can do a faux cell phone exchange with no one on the other end. Choose your words carefully—note that women who like to go out to wild parties are fond of calling each other "babe" and "sweetie." So say things like, "Okay, babe, meet you at the club at ten!" Your mom will love your new term of endearment for her.

Photoshop and Facebook

You can also broadcast your awesome weekend after the fact through Photoshopped pics posted on Facebook. Put you and your girlfriends in all sorts of crazy scenarios—doing shots off some guy's abs, doing shots off a rhinoceros's horn, doing shots off a newborn baby's head (careful of the soft spot!). This strategy is sort of situation-specific, though—you can't stop the nerdy guy in IT from asking you out today by showing him a Facebook photo from the future. But you can always tell him you're going out with your friends, and then he'll see the proof that you did it. He'll also see that you are a wild and crazy creature and that he clearly has no shot.

Doing Work from Home

The truth is, your company is the kind of place where you're actually glad to show up every day—or not show up. Because you have a long, painful commute, your boss actually lets you have two days a week to "work from home." It's this kind of flexibility and trust in your work ethic that makes you a happy and dedicated member of the team. If only more employers would stop hovering and entrust employees with the freedom to make their own schedules, there would be a much happier work force overall.

Of course, we all know that "work from home" really means "eat choco-late Cheerios in your pajamas while watching *Simpsons* episodes all day."

Wait—that's not really fair. It doesn't always mean that. Sometimes, it means "go to the beach, lie around and get fried by the sun while eating curly cheese fries until 5:00 P.M."

But you don't want your *boss* to know that especially since your company is so cool and flexible about that stuff. You need to present the illusion that you are actually having something resembling a normal workday from your home. This work-from-home thing is just too awesome to screw up!

Send Scheduled E-mails

Did you know that you don't have to be at your desk—or even on your smart phone—to send e-mails during the slavish hours of nine to five? There are apps, such as Boomerang for Gmail, that allow you to schedule messages for hours, days, even up to a month in advance. So if you would like to turn in an assignment or update your boss on a certain project, but would really rather take a nice long nap in front of the TV at that time, just schedule your e-mail to be sent at the designated time and nap away.

Did I say nine to five? Why restrict yourself to normal working hours? We all know you can be *so* much more productive if you start working at 6:00 A.M.! Schedule a whole slew of e-mails to be sent at 6:00 A.M., and you will look like the most ambitious, early bird freak on the planet! People will get to their desks at 8:00 A.M. and feel sheepish because of you! Way to go!

Of course, in order to keep up with the responses to these messages, you will need to check your e-mail at some point in the day. But checking e-mail a few times a day is a lot better than actually monitoring your incoming messages all day long like you're at work!

Save Up Work from Previous Days

When you're actually at the office, you don't *always* have to produce a final product to convince your boss you are working—just shuffling papers and typing a lot can do that job pretty well (see: "Having a Productive Day"). However, when you're working from home, you can shuffle all the papers you want and type until your fingers are numb, but if your boss can't see it, it doesn't count.

Nope, you should save the shuffling and typing for when it can be seen, and stockpile your actual output for work-from-home days. That way, you can turn in a bunch of stuff on those days even while you're watching old *Rocky & Bullwinkle* cartoons. It will look like you're even *more* productive on work-from-home days than on shuffle-and-type days!

Okay, the truth is, you're going to have to break down and work at some point during the week, otherwise, the stuff is never going to get done. But if you work smart, not hard, you can still have plenty of time leftover to do nothing at all.

Having "Nerdy" Interests to Sound Smarter In Front Of Coworkers

Back in junior high, you were a complete and total nerd—you had a bright pink retainer, a female mullet (femullet), and a passion for Brontë sisters' novels. Oh, and *opera*. And *bug collecting*, for the love of god. Each interest of yours was more socially unacceptable than the last. You were just plain weird—in other words, a true original. You were a nerd down to your odd little core.

Over the years, you learned to stuff that originality down. You allowed the sides of your hair to grow back and put your dead bugs in a drawer for safekeeping. You traded in opera, first for pop music, and then for "alternative" music, all as the cultural whims demanded.

You worked and worked to become "normal," and by the time you finished college and were unleashed on the workforce, you were—mostly. Today, you're a beautiful woman who is fashionable, interesting, and successful.

The problem? It seems that your coworkers—particularly the male ones—don't take you quite as seriously as they do the office's resident "geek girl." This girl, whom everyone calls "*adorkable*," wears big, in-your-face glasses, spews out *Star Trek* movie references, and claims to love science fiction novels and *World of Warcraft*. WTF? It seems that you're now viewed as some sort of froufrou prom queen, while nerd girl here is seen as a super smart, all-around cool chick. What the hell happened?

Be Into Sci-Fi

Although being nerdy is über trendy these days, you can't just be any old nerd. You need to be a sci-fi nerd. Oh, and I almost forgot—a *hot* sci-fi nerd. It seems as though hot women who pretend to love *Star Trek* and zombies are the coolest creatures imaginable.

From what I can tell, this "fake nerd" trend began with young Hollywood actresses wanting to make a big blockbuster science fiction movie and get rich. In order to achieve this, these beautiful young things had to pander to some of the dorkiest dorks on the planet—male movie reviewers. This phenomenon, in turn, has spread out into the culture at large, with beautiful women feeling the need to show off their "nerd cred." This means going to geek conventions like Comic-Con, pretending to love *Star Trek*, and playing Dungeons & Dragons. Sadly, other female nerds—ones who love literature, opera, or bugs—are still pretty much invisible. So are nerds who are generally unsexy.

Warning: They Are Onto You

I would be remiss if I didn't give you ladies the heads-up that the nerds have been catching on to your little act. In doing some diligent Internet research on the topic, I came across *many, many* posts from nerd men complaining about "hot women pretending to be nerds." We all know that nerds run the Internet, so if it's there, it's everywhere. I won't even address the unmitigated nerve these nerds have to actually be *complaining* about hot women trying to kiss up to them when they should thank sweet baby Jesus that any woman would even give them the time of day (the time of day, BTW, is sixteen minutes past dork o'clock—oops!—your fifteen minutes just ended, nerd boys). What I am saying to the ladies is that to pull off this nerd girl thing, you're really going to have to be on top of your game. If you are going to bring up how much you love the Avengers, you had better know that Loki is Thor's adopted brother, and that the Avengers-Defenders war storyline was introduced in *Avengers* #115. In other words, you're going to have to out-nerd these nerds, and who really has time for that?

Maybe I'm alone in this, but I don't really think these comic book nerds seem all that intelligent. I say the best nerdy interest to have is reading, whatever the genre. Reading the classics will score you points with literary types; or you can subscribe to the *New Yorker* ("New York," BTW, is the noncomic nerd name for Gotham City).

An Appointment to Get Out of a Meeting or Leave Work Early

Your week has been nothing but back-to-back meetings—meetings about current work projects, meetings about when to have another meeting, meetings about whether maybe your company has too many meetings (the answer: no way!). The hilarious part—if it didn't also make you want to cry—is that rather than sitting in a meeting talking about these projects, you could be at your desk actually *working* on them. Instead, you've been doodling what you hope will someday be artistic masterpieces that will enable you to quit your job.

In fact, there's a meeting scheduled for this afternoon, in which you are supposed to report to the higher-ups about how one of your projects is coming along. The truth is, it's *not* coming along, because almost every waking hour of your recent history has been sucked up into meetings. You would think they would somehow understand this, but they don't. You're beginning to suspect that these meeting freaks have discovered a traversable wormhole through which they are able to go back in time. It's totally unfair that they haven't shared this with you.

Regardless, your meeting is on the books for 2:00 P.M., and you're just not ready. You need to bust out of this place for the day—but you have to fake it convincingly.

Use an App!

Yes, of course there are apps for getting out of meetings—are you really surprised? One of them, specifically for business meetings, allows you to schedule an "emergency text" to come in at a certain time. You can just read the text and say, "Oops! It seems my hot water heater exploded and my apartment is flooded. I have to go take care of that." Another service interrupts you with an urgent phone call, which will provide a recorded "repeat after me" voice telling you exactly which words to utter. You'll be fed lines like, "Oh my god. Where are you right now?" and, "Okay, calm down. I'll be right there." It's better than having to come up with your own impromptu dialogue in front of your boss and colleagues. Many of these services are cheap or free, so go for it—but use it sparingly, or they *will* catch on to you.

Use Kids and Pets

Another valuable get-out-of-jail-free card is your precious child. It's true, children are not put on this earth so that we can use them to weasel out of unpleasant work situations, but this is definitely a perk of having them. A last-minute sick kid who needs to be picked up at school is an ironclad reason for you to duck out of that meeting. Even better is a kid who gets in trouble at school. See, most parents are embarrassed to say their child is a disciplinary problem and therefore would hesitate to use this—even if it were the truth. Therefore, no one would expect you to *falsely accuse your child* of being sent home for bad behavior. No good parent would throw her kid under the bus that way! That's why you can do it and get away with it. You can later explain that your child has been acting out due to all of the work meetings that have taken up your time!

Of course, not everyone has kids, so this excuse might wear thin for the nonprocreators on the board of directors. In such cases, you still have a shot at appealing to their sympathies—have a cat emergency. Informal studies (done by me, of my friends and associates) have found that if a person doesn't have children, she probably has a cat. And people who have cats instead of kids really love those cats. A lot. So all you have to do in this case is have a cat health emergency come up and have to take Mittens in to the vet office. If your boss doesn't even have a cat, I don't know what to do for you. Work harder on those doodles, Picasso!

Job Experience During an Interview

Hooray! You've been called in for an interview for a job you know you would love and that you are pretty sure you'd be great at. The job's meant for you, and you are meant for it—it's true love! Now it's just a matter of convincing this intimidatingly tall, perfectly coiffed hiring manager not to stand between you and your true love.

Why would she do that? Well, if we're being honest here, you don't exactly have the precise work experience that the job calls for. In fact, you've had maybe one job in this particular field, and the rest of it has been a series of proverbial "odd jobs." Some of them have been truly odd, too—dressing up as Barney the dinosaur for kids' parties, being a hair washer at a salon, renting yourself out as a human guinea pig for pharmaceutical drug trials, and of course, writing fortune cookies.

But don't be discouraged. You might not have experience in the field, but you may very well have the skill set the job requires. For example, you're a self-starter, you're able to work independently, you have excellent people skills, and you're comfortable in a fast-paced environment. So, why should it matter how you acquired these skills? A wise man once said, "There is more than one journey toward any destination." Actually, you wrote that for a fortune cookie once.

Market Your "Brand"

The fact that you've been brought in for an interview is a very encouraging sign. Obviously, these people saw something on your resume that prompted them to make time in their schedules to meet you. For this reason, you should focus more on being personable and charming than on whatever's missing from your job history. Remember, they've already seen your resume and they called you anyway. What they haven't seen is *you*. So show them some you! Make sure you look like a million bucks or at least a hundred thousand. Smile and let your personality show, but keep it professional. It's great to showcase your wit and charm, but don't try to turn this thing into a one-woman monologue. Keep it succinct and let the interviewer control the direction and the pace of the conversation.

Don't Overexplain Yourself

You might feel compelled to justify your lack of relevant job experience. All I can say is *don't do it*. You don't need to address this topic unless they bring it up. Do *not* offer lengthy or unrequested explanations for any gaps or oddities in your resume. In fact, I'd say for life in general, *overexplaining yourself is a horrible idea*, no matter how tempting it is. It's like a rabbit hole of insecurity that you'll only fall deeper and deeper into. Next thing you know, you'll want to explain why you're explaining so much, and so on, and so on, until they call those nice men to escort you out.

Use What You Have

As I mentioned previously, there's more than one way to skin a cat, although if you ever had a job as a cat skinner, I don't ever want to talk to you again.

The point is, whether you know it or not, you do have a skill set. It doesn't matter if the jobs you've had were weird, they taught you something. Dressing up as Barney for kids' parties gave you skills in entertainment, party planning, and self-motivation. Plus, there were some muffled communication skills involved, not to mention the fast-paced environment. (Boy, did you have to move fast to avoid those kids trying to kick you!) Being a human guinea pig taught you to take risks, and writing fortune cookies taught you innovation and intuition. A job as a janitor teaches organization and attention to detail, and a pool lifeguard teaches how to look good in sunglasses while pretending to watch kids. Believe me, this is a skill you'll need as a parent!

CHAPTER FIVE

Pulling a Betty Crocker

Ah, Betty Crocker—now *there* was the perfect homemaker. You picture her as apple pie-cheeked and Fourth of July eyed, the essence of apron-clad natural beauty. She spent her days blowing kisses, cooling pies, and whisking—lots of whisking—and the result was delicious baked goods and wholesome meals, made with love and a dollop of Americana. She did all of this without effort, without stress, without a microwave.

Betty's enough to make you feel like a real jerk when you rush home from work, feed your children those awful KFC "Everything We Sell, Mashed Up and Crammed Into a Bowl" bowls (no whisking needed), and rush off to a PTA meeting. Why are you such a loser, when Betty was so amazing and perfect?

Here's why—Betty was a total fake. The woman never existed.

"Betty Crocker" was a name concocted by some suits at the *Fortune 500* Company General Mills. They chose the first name "Betty" because it sounded "cheery," and the last name "Crocker," because she was a crock. (Okay, I lie. It was some company exec's name.) This fake person proceeded to crank out cookbooks, cake mixes, and all kinds of unfairly heightened expectations for flesh-and-blood females.

Why should you have to be Betty Crocker when not even Betty Crocker has to be Betty Crocker? You don't! If corporate bigwigs faked Betty, you can fake your own domestic goddess!

This section includes all sorts of sneaky strategies for appearing put-together, inspired, and flawless in the domestic realm. From vandalizing store-bought cupcakes for a "homemade" effect to faking tolerance for your kids' bratty friends, here are tricks to go from faux-maker to home-maker. Because really, "home" is where the heart is—and Betty Crocker, you don't even have a chest cavity.

A Clean Bathroom and Immaculate Kitchen When Unexpected Guests Arrive

If your house or apartment were a person, it would be a person with a severe stomach virus, because it's throwing up all over itself. (Or are you purging, little house? Don't you know you're far too small already?) Your kitchen table is spewing old electric bills and coupon circulars so out-dated they've practically recycled themselves out of embarrassment. Not to mention those mysterious refrigerator items so furry that you suspect they now have central nervous systems. Then there's the bathroom—a nightmare of lint, your husband's facial hair, and formerly clean soap that has been utterly debauched into no-good "scum."

And guess what? Some last-minute guests are dropping in for a visit!

It's understandable that your first instinct is to discreetly murder your guests and hide them in your fridge with the furry undesirables. But that is not polite, and it will really only make your house messier.

Die, Soap Scum!

I feel it is necessary to make special mention of the bathroom, since it is the only room of the house where your guests have the privacy to inspect its cleanliness to their nosy hearts' content. Unlike the other rooms of the house, you can't follow them into the bathroom and distract them with another drink or a compliment for their dress. You have to stand there, helpless, while they close the door and examine your personal hygiene room. Yay!

Blogger Anna Moseley, of *www.askannamoseley.com*, suggests doing an emergency bathroom fake with the help of some Clorox wipes, a dispenser of hand soap, and your fingernails. First, she recommends pouring one pump of hand soap into the sink, turning on the water, and using your hand to wipe down the sink. Use your fingernails to scrape any stubborn soap scum away. Then use one Clorox wipe to clean the surfaces of your toilet and another to wipe any hair or lint from the floor. Finally, replace your old hand towel with a clean one.

Because I am paranoid, I would additionally advise removing any potentially embarrassing medications or ointments from your medicine cabinet and emptying the wastebasket. You never know how far people might go to dig up some "dirt" on you.

Fridge Monsters and More

The kitchen, it seems, comes right after the bathroom as far as being a potential source of ickiness and subsequent judgment. People like to know their food is being prepared in an *E. Coli*–free environment. You can reassure your guests on this front by doing a quick cleanup job—and by purchasing food prepared elsewhere!

First, according to Sarah Aguirre at *http://housekeeping.about.com*, make sure your dishwasher situation is under control. If you have a dishwasher full of dirty dishes, run the cycle and put them away. If there's no time for that, you'll need to put them in a large box and hide them temporarily.

To eliminate clutter such as bills and other paper, use the "Box and Banish" method recommended by Cynthia Ewer at *www.organizedhome.com*. Gather these items into a box, and stuff them into a cabinet or closet for the day. (No, unfortunately, you cannot "box and banish" your uninvited guests.)

Next, Aguirre says to rinse out your sponges and washrags, and put any dirty ones in with your dirty laundry. Then wipe down the sink and counters, just for visible and obvious dirt. Don't worry about details like the inside of the microwave—just close the door. For your floor, you'll want to sweep thoroughly and dry mop.

Finally, it's time to face the fridge monsters, and anything else that might give your house that not-so-fresh feeling. Burn some potpourri or cinnamon sticks on the stove, and get rid of anything that festers (other than your husband).

Now, sit down, relax, and have a drink. Welcome, unwelcome guests!

A Homemade Bake Sale Item for a Fundraiser

Listen, Missy. You are insane. You work a crazy full-time job for a boss who's borderline OCD, you're married to a man who is *definitely* ADD, and you have *four* kids—OMFG! Add to that a dog with irritable bowel syndrome, and you have possibly the most chaotic, high-maintenance and acronym-riddled life anyone could possibly invent. Congratulations?

As if this weren't enough, you've volunteered to be a room mother for your kids' classes. Way to go, genius! It wasn't enough for you to be the mother of four kids and a gassy dog—you have to be the mother of a whole room? Let's just do some fast math—assuming there are about twenty kids in each child's class, that's eighty kids you're "mothering." Hmm, pretty soon it might be time to move into that giant shoe . . .

Anyway, it turns out that one of your kids' grades is having a bake sale to benefit the school—like, tomorrow. You know this only because the letter requesting baked goods from all room moms was discovered wadded and crumpled in the pocket of your daughter's jeans in the wash.

This is impossible. If you had time to lovingly bake a batch of homemade cupcakes, you'd also have time to get your roots done, and since said roots look like a cross between a skunk and an off-the-wagon Lindsay Lohan, you clearly have not had that kind of time. Time for some bakery fakery!

Cookie Cut

Ironically, in order to preserve the image of you as the perfect wife/ mom/workplace dynamo/room mother, you have to deliberately create imperfections in your bakery-bought confections. Jessie Moore Oleson, of *www.cakespy.com*, says that cookies, cupcakes, or cakes that look "too perfect" are a dead giveaway that you purchased them. So your job is to rough these baked goods up a bit, so that everyone knows how you slaved over them.

For cookies, perfect symmetry of shape and a lack of overdone or browned bottoms might cause people to think, "store-bought." So Moore Oleson advises the following fix: Put a pat of butter in a frying pan on medium heat, and while you wait for the butter to melt and bubble, use a knife to file gently away at the edges of your cookies. Then place them on the skillet and leave them on until they brown on the bottom. Then remove them, and use your hands to slightly dent the tops and sides to look "homemade." Tip: Don't completely mash or destroy them, or they will look like they were homemade by an insane baby. Another way to add a homemade touch is to add your own decorative flourishes to the cookies. You can use sprinkles, shredded coconut, glaze, or whatever you want—just keep it "real," a.k.a., random!

Cupcake De-Icing

Moore Oleson rightly points out that the biggest problem with store bought cupcakes is that ridiculously beautiful way they're decorated. That's fair enough; professional bakers and cake decorators take pride in their art. They want to show how much better they make a cupcake look than us mere amateurs. Sure, that's great, but you want these cupcakes to look like the creations of an amateur (an amateur *superwoman*, that is). So your job is to totally *undo* the decorator's beautiful work. They won't ever need to know!

Suppose, for example, that a professional pastry dispenser has doled out the icing on your cupcakes in those flawless little poufs. You need to flatten and level those gorgeous, sugary rosettes before they rat you out. Moore Oleson advises using a butter knife to gently spread the frosting out into more old-school, flawed coverage. Maybe even add some of your own sprinkles to make it look like traditional "room mother" fare. Sure, it won't look as good, but that's the point. It will *taste* awesome, however.

PS, if anyone asks you for a recipe, Moore Oleson says you can non-committally agree to e-mail it, but never follow up. Hopefully, if you uglify your baked goods enough, no one will even realize their awesomeness until you're long gone!

A Tidy Car on Carpool Day

You are such an awesome, responsible human; not only is your house super green with compact fluorescent light bulbs and eco-friendly cleaning supplies, you also are one of the first people you know to own a hybrid vehicle. And recently, you've organized an office carpool for nearby coworkers. You're all saving money on gas, reducing nasty toxic emissions, and decreasing traffic and subsequent nut-case road rage (especially by reducing your coworker Angry Carl's time behind the wheel). Thanks to you, the world is safer, and the air is cleaner.

Too bad your *car* isn't cleaner. Because today, it turns out, is your day for transporting the gang to the office, and unfortunately, your hybrid looks like a hybrid between a car and the city dump. There are month-old fruit rollups that now look like dehydrated tongues, assorted receipts that probably contain itemized humiliation (extra absorbency tampons, $5.95; Save-A-Lot brand stool softener, $4.50; Bunion Care Gel Sleeve, $11.95; Doritos $4.95), and a veritable sea of Goldfish Crackers scattered all over the interior. This is not even to mention the broken sunglasses, dog hair, and random small change wedged between the seats.

Did I mention dog hair? How about dog smell? And kid smell?

You need to fake it quick, Enviro-Girl! Because what's the use of cleaner air outside the car if the air *inside* the car is vile? You've got about an hour, so let the faking begin!

Hide the Clutter

Your first step in reducing your car's chances of appearing on *Hoarders: "Car Edition"* is to remove all the junk and clutter. Simply grab one trash bag and one box for storage. Everything that is trash (yes, sorry, but the fruit rollup jerky does qualify) goes right into the bag, and everything else goes into the box. You can store the box in your garage, or even in the trunk like some shameful corpse you're hiding. If you don't feel as though you have time to make these life-altering decisions about "trash vs. nontrash," you can just put everything in the box for now. But seriously, maybe you really are a car hoarder.

Blanket Statement

You probably don't have time for a full car vacuum or to go to a car wash to have the interior vacuumed for you. If you do have time for either of these, go for it! If not, don't worry: You can implement a quick fix.

Simply drape blankets on the seats to cover up any stains, hairs, or other funky items that might not be easily removable. Your passengers might wonder why there are blankets on the seats, but they also probably won't *really* want to know. So respect the part of them that doesn't want to know and don't tell them. If they start annoying you with questions, tell them you use the blankets to conceal the bodies of your victims prior to dumping them in the ocean. That'll bring the conversation (and probably the carpool) to a halt.

If the whole blanket scenario seems a bit too rustic for you, some car manufacturers also sell seat covers for the very purpose of covering stains *and* protecting your car from future messes. Plus, everyone knows how hard it is to wrap a body in a car seat cover!

New Car Smell

The final step for making your car acceptable for carpool day is to freshen up that smell. There are now a ton of different types of air fresheners available for cars—you don't have to have a whole forest of those "little trees" anymore. There are sprays, gels, plug-ins, "fragrance cartridges," cans, and vent clips. You can get your car to smell like everything from candy to "fresh laundry." Although why would you be doing laundry in your car? Do you, like, live there or something?

Patience with the Kids in Your Family

It's barely 7:00 A.M. on a Saturday, and your kids have already microwaved a light bulb, taped your scrapbooking project onto the dog, and written out gang slogans using alphabet soup (in a way, you're oddly proud that they can spell, "Mess with the best, die like the rest"). Now they're jumping on your bed, making the whole thing shake like the bed in *The*

Exorcist on steroids. They want you to tell them a story. "Once upon a time," you say, "Mommy used to do this thing called sleep . . ."

But of course, they don't want to hear *that* story—that's *so* boring! Wake up and smell the microwaved glass shards, Mom—Once Upon a Time is over.

It's very difficult to maintain your patience and be a good role model when your kids are driving your household to the brink of madness. (No, I mean they're literally driving—that's them rolling out of the driveway, headed toward said brink. Hurry up and stop them!) But if you take a few minutes to step back, breathe deeply, and try to get inside their crazy little minds, you can spare everyone the sight of Mommy's nervous breakdown.

Kids: Not Guilty by Reason of Insanity

When considering your kids' bizarre behavior, let's look to the example of our criminal justice system. Insane people tend to be punished differently, because they are not able to fully distinguish between right and wrong. And let's face it—all kids are kind of insane. Even the best-behaved child might all of a sudden decide he/she want to eat cat food or try to iron silly putty. And then they actually *do it*. What adult—living outside a rubber room—does such things?

Kids exist in a prolonged state of temporary insanity—they haven't yet developed impulse control or adult morality. It's our job as parents to slowly rehabilitate them and eventually make them sane enough to release into the world. We have to teach them right from wrong, but we also have to realize they're not going to get this concept on the first try. Or even the thousandth.

Take a Fake-cation

Just like any other situation involving prolonged dealings with crazy people, being a parent can sometimes make you want to pull your hair out. But try not to—you'd look pretty weird without hair. Besides, you want to model rational behavior and self-control, so freaking out is not a good choice. When your emotions reach a fever pitch and you feel like you're going to go over the edge, take a break. Walk away for a minute. Close your eyes, take a deep breath, and transport yourself to a beautiful, aquamarine beach in Jamaica. Picture yourself swaying back and forth on a hammock suspended between two palm trees. Allow yourself to be perfectly at ease. They'll still be eating clay when you open your eyes, but you'll be able to face it with a calmer attitude.

Be the Grownup

Once you get yourself through the crisis without losing your temper, you can gently but firmly explain to your kids why their behavior is straitjacket crazy. Tell them that clay is not only a socially frowned-upon food, but also a gastrointestinal nightmare. (If you really want to impress them, you can teach them the word "geophagy," which basically means "eating clay.") And be sure to impose consequences, such as, "If you eat the clay, it gets taken away." (Note: Not all consequences lend themselves so easily to Johnnie Cochran-esque rhymes, especially if the offense involves a rhinoceros or an orange.)

The point being, you want to demonstrate calmness, self-control, and consequences. They might be little crazy-heads now, but if you teach them well, they will get better eventually. And the truth is, someone has to be the grownup, and since you're a few decades their senior, I nominate you. You know you love them, alphabet soup graffiti and all!

Being Santa Claus, the Easter Bunny, and the Tooth Fairy

Even for those of us who try to live a life free of fakery and deception, one inevitable truth remains: A large number of us will eventually have to pretend to be an obese saint, a mutant rabbit, or a winged entity with an insatiable greed for temporary molars. (What does she even *do* with them, anyway? Creepy.) So even if you've been a goody-goody for most of your existence, you will end up having to dish out some of the most absurd and improbable lies you've ever heard to your own kids. You know, the same lies your parents told you, the ones that caused you such disillusionment and psychic pain when you saw what a sham they were. Ah, childhood—it's so magical!

What's your choice, though, really? You could be that one super PC mom who decides to empower her children with the truth, also known as "the least popular mom on the block." You don't want to be a wet blanket, do you? Life is filled with painful realities, most of which your children will uncover in due time. Let them at least have the aging home intruder, the ginormous rodent and the tooth-buying weirdo.

Lean on Your "Helpers"

Among the first flaws your kids are likely to find in the Santa Claus/Easter Bunny farce are the shoddy impersonators seen at department stores, Moose lodges, or local parades. Often, these are out-of-work actors, college kids working for minimum wage, or that crazy old man in town whose jolliness may or may not come directly from a flask of Jack Daniel's.

Your child might ask, "Why did Santa's beard fall off while I was talking to him?" or "Why could I see a person's eyes inside the Easter Bunny's head? or "Why does Santa's breath smell like Nick Nolte after a rough night?"

At first you might panic, but don't. Just rely on the "helper explanation." Tell your children that these aren't the *real* Santa or Easter Bunny, but local helpers who dress up as their likeness. Sort of like celebrity look-alikes, they represent the real Santa or the Easter Bunny because they couldn't be everywhere at once. Just like Elvis.

Create Your Own Character

Another huge problem in faking Santa or the Easter Bunny is the fact that these fictional characters vary wildly from household to household. You will begin to hear, "At Braden's house, Santa leaves a note," or "The Easter Bunny gives Sophia chocolate-covered bacon," or "Nathaniel gets $150 per tooth in large bills." Explain that for each family, the tradition is different and that the lovable givers in question treat each child individually. Tell your child that the Easter Bunny knows that sugar-coated breakfast meats make them hyper, that Santa Claus has really bad handwriting, and the tooth fairy spent so much on Nathaniel that now she's broke.

Keep the Magic Alive

The truth is, we live in a world where "magic" is a retired basketball player and "wonder" is a kind of white bread that's horrible for you. If your kids are lucky enough to believe in Santa, the Easter Bunny, and the tooth fairy for a while, let them. Sure, it's all a big act, but it's an act that will make their little faces light up with anticipation and joy.

They might be disappointed when they first realize they've been tricked, but usually, by that time, they're ready to let go. With the tooth fairy, there's actually a developmental cutoff to kids losing teeth (about age ten), so they literally grow out of it. Unless, of course, they turn into maladjusted, thirty-something adults who intentionally dislodge their own teeth in order to extort their parents (thanks for the check, Mom!).

A Homemade Meal When You Haven't Been Home All Day

It has been one of those annoying "hurry up and wait" days—those frustrating combinations of panic and drudgery that leave you unsure whether to reach for your antidepressant or your anxiety meds. First, you rush into work just to sit in a conference room, waiting for your boss to show up for an early meeting. Then you hurry back to your desk to call a client for a scheduled phone call, and wait on hold, listening to Rod Stewart ballads (yes, he *has* told you lately that he loves you, the last time this stupid song came on). At lunchtime, you hurry to the DMV to renew your license, and wait in a long line of annoyed people to have a terribly unflattering picture taken.

As if that wasn't bad enough, tonight you're entertaining a few other couples for dinner, so you hurry to your car, wait in traffic, hurry home and wait for your glacier-slow oven to preheat. You have a delicious recipe you plan to make—roasted chicken with rosemary potatoes. Then you take a closer look and realize that instead of needing to cook for 20 minutes, this dish needs to cook for 200 minutes! Oh, and you forgot to even take the bird out of the freezer to defrost. Unfortunately, your guests are coming in an hour, so "hurry up and wait" isn't going to cut it. Just "hurry up!"

Hit the Grocery Deli

According to *http://ideas.thenest.com*, the deli department of your local grocery store is the best friend you can have when faking a home cooked meal—unless your dinner guests are such awesome friends that you can tell them this whole ridiculous story, and they will just laugh and give you lots of big hugs (but for now, just stick with that deli).

Most grocery stores provide a wide array of freshly made meats and side dishes, such as roasted chicken, fish, or beef. And many will even broil up some salmon or chicken for you on the spot. How cool is that? Literally, someone is cooking your dinner for you. So pick something delicious and maybe even healthy, and grab some yummy side dishes while you're at it. Editors at *http://ideas.thenest.com* also advise picking up a loaf of good bread and a bagged salad. Just throw in some plum or cherry tomatoes, some dressing, and maybe some croutons, cheese, or other flourishes.

Seriously, your kids could probably make this salad. And if they're good kids who know how to earn their keep, maybe they should. After all, you need time to fake your makeup, hair, and clothes! As a reward, offer them the leftovers of the delicious store-bought dessert you picked up.

Add Your Personal Touch

The next step, once you get the food home, is to remove any and all signs of "store-boughtness," including packaging, labels, nutrition information, and "Day Old/Half Off Sale" stickers. You must undo all their efforts to make the food look professionally made. The editors suggest maybe adding a garnish, such as a sprig of parsley, or some of your own herbs. If you're serving something like fried chicken, you can put it on a bed of lettuce. For grilled chicken or fish, you might choose to add a topping of salsa or pesto. According to editors at *http://ideas.thenest.com*, a piece of cooked, glazed salmon can be dressed up with some noodles and Asian dressing. Adding little items from your own pantry will definitely add to the illusion of a home cooked meal. Just serve them on your best plates, open a bottle of wine or two, and voilà! Hurry up and wait for the compliments to come pouring in!

Knowing How to Solve a Homework Assignment

Your kid has a big book report due on the use of allegory in George Orwell's *Animal Farm.* Or perhaps he's supposed to make a functioning volcano like Peter Brady on that episode of *The Brady Bunch* where the volcano erupts all over Marcia and her snobby friends. Or maybe she has five pages of geometry homework—isosceles triangles, conic solids, and null sets—that make you break into a cold sweat. It's enough to make *you* feel like a "null set."

Look, you are a highly educated person, with a bachelor's degree in English and a master's degree in something else. You just happen to not have retained half of the stuff you learned in fifth grade. Hey, don't they say all the important stuff was covered in kindergarten?

It wasn't always like this. At one time, you used to be a whiz at helping them with their homework. You're a great speller, and your coloring skills are kick-ass. But now it seems as though your kids have officially reached the point where their homework assignments present a genuine challenge. Your kid is frustrated, and so are you. And the dog is looking awfully hungry for some workbook pages. Hmm, that would make everyone happy, wouldn't it?

Delegate Appropriately

According to Amanda Waas at *www.rachaelraymag.com*, one smart way to be helpful to your children with homework assignments is to recognize which parent is right for what job. If you know you're not into messy projects, you might want to recruit your husband for the volcano project. Guys love building things, especially things that are potentially messy, destructive, or even remotely phallic.

Seriously, though, working as a team on homework assignments is a great way to not only help your kids academically, but encourage plenty of one-on-one time with both parents. And your husband will appreciate the chance to feel important, powerful, and strong . . . just like a volcano!

Don't Fear Math

For many of us, women especially, the most terrifying horror movie would be about a knife-wielding radical exponent trying to trapezoid people and bisect them into fractions. It's some disturbing stuff, for sure. No one gets out alive!

But just because you've always struggled with math doesn't mean you should continue to be haunted by the stuff. Believe it or not, some people who had a terrible time with math as kids have gone on to become math teachers! And helping out with a grade school math assignment might be a good way to ease into facing your fear. What I'm saying is, don't rule yourself out as a potential math helper. Your empathy might actually be a good thing if your child is struggling. The two of you can learn together.

Consult the Internet

When it comes to homework, there's this awesome thing that wasn't around back when you were a kid—the Internet. How easy these kids have it! But when it comes to homework, kids having it easy equals Mom having it easy. So, if you don't know how to help your kid out with a specific problem, why not Google it? The Internet is like a library that's right there all the time, but it doesn't have that stern-faced old librarian Mrs. Kunkler giving you judgmental looks when you try to check out *Are You There God? It's Me, Margaret!* You can do your independent research without being embarrassed and encourage your child to learn independently, too—though not necessarily about getting his period!

Clean Clothes When You Haven't Had Time to Do Laundry

Aw, look at you and your family—you're like a Sears catalog! All dressed in nice, crisply creased, freshly laundered clothes. You all look like a bunch of hired models—even the dog's preppie turtleneck is clean as he plays Frisbee with your preppie turtleneck-clad husband. Your kids are frolicking around in perfect kid outfits, laughing gleefully in their seersucker loungewear and kid-model sandals. They manage to happily enjoy a rousing game of tag while somehow keeping their clothing pristine. What a family!

Of course, all good things must end, and this refreshingly clean family thing is due to end any minute now. See, you've been so busy and stressed this week you've barely had time to inhale necessary and lifesaving air, let alone do laundry for your family. These gorgeous catalog-ready outfits happen to be the last of the clean clothes in your entire house. Only you know that underneath those turtlenecks, you and your family are soon-to-be rednecks.

Oh, snap! What's that going on over there? Looks like your Sears catalog dog is rolling around in rabbit feces. In his handsome turtleneck! Not to mention his fur coat, which is kind of a daily outfit he can't even take off. Oh, and now your kids are following suit—in their seersucker suits. You've got to fake some clean clothes, fast!

Buy New Clothes

If you happen to have a fair amount of disposable income, you can have what I affectionately call "disposable clothes." Not really disposable—you don't want to actually throw your dirty clothes out—but you can use them as a great excuse to go shopping for some new clothes! Just put the icky stuff in the hamper and hit the mall, where you can outfit your entire family in brand new, clean items. If you happen to be one of those people who feel the need to wash brand new clothes before you wear them, I'm sorry to report that you're doomed either way. I would also point out that if you have time to go shopping, you probably have time to wash clothes. Sorry, just saying.

Febreze It!

For any clothes that don't have visible stains or don't smell horrendous, you might have the option of spraying them with Febreze and letting them tumble in the dryer for a while. Writers at *www.mancouch.com* offer this solution for artificially freshening up your dirty clothes and allowing them to make a repeat performance in your clothing rotation. However, clothes with difficult or stubborn stains (kids' clothes) or those that might be the victims of heavy perspiration (men's clothes), this might not be quite enough. I'm not sure it's cool to spray your dog with Febreze either. So basically, Febreze probably works best if you are a female who sweats minimally, does not spill juice boxes on herself, and is not a member of the canine species. No offense to any bitches who may be reading this book for tips—I love dogs! I'm just not sure I can help you to faux-launder yourself.

Wash and Fold Service

Theoretically, you could take your clothes to the Laundromat, but who has time to sit around trying to find coins and waiting for your clothes to be done? If you had that kind of time, you'd wash them yourself.

But here's a brilliant factoid: Quite a few Laundromats also offer a "wash and fold" service, where you can get a load of laundry washed, dried, *and* folded by the Laundromat employees. Most of these services charge by the pound of laundry. The beauty is that you can drop off your family's nasty clothes and have them washed, dried and folded while you do other necessary stuff. Again, your dog cannot undergo this service, as you certainly would not want him or her to come back folded.

Liking the Gifts Your Family Got You

Happy Mother's Day or Happy Birthday to you, lady! It's another special day with your awesome husband and kids, another occasion for them to celebrate who you are and what you mean to them. Unfortunately, as you're discovering through their year's worth of gifts to you, "who you are" includes the following: Pusher of Vacuum Apparatus (bagless vacuum to celebrate your motherly duties, from husband); Mother of Four Who Desperately Needs to Exercise Her Flabby, Repulsive Turkey Neck (portable neckline slimming exerciser, from your kids); Wife in Need of Respiration-Constricting Lingerie That Also Manages to Depict Your Codependent/Caretaking Dynamic (skin-tight nurse uniform monstrosity, from husband); Person Who Obviously Needs to Give Just a Little Bit More, Even on Their Birthday, Until It Really, Really Hurts (donation to charity given in your name, from those sweet kids of yours).

Wow. Talk about some lame gifts! You've almost started to dread the holidays that are supposed to be "about you," because usually they're about you pretending to be delighted by gifts that make you want to regift your entire clan.

You're not ungrateful, really! It's just that you give, and give, and give, all year round. It would be nice if just for these few days, you could receive something awesome.

Don't Turn Gifts Into a Test

We all know at least one person who treats gift giving as an unofficial test of love, devotion, respect, or any of those other emotions Hallmark clearly invented. Maybe you are that person. The reality is, gifts aren't a test—they're just gifts. Ideally, we give gifts freely out of love, and accept them gratefully out of love. Sitting around wondering if your husband is going to "get it right" this time is a quick way to end up being very disappointed. So, maybe he gives you a washing machine for Christmas. It's not the most romantic gift, but maybe he was trying to make life easier for you. Or maybe he commits the common male crime of giving you lingerie. Just think—there are women who don't have a guy who *wants* to see them in lingerie. Say your kids' gift of a neck exerciser is unintentionally insulting. You might be thankful later, when yours is the only buff neck among your loose-wattled friends. The point here is that you love your family, and they love you. They've already passed the test. Everything beyond that is a bonus.

Be Nicer to Yourself

It has been my observation that women who place the most emphasis on gifts are those who don't treat themselves right. They are almost martyr-like in their unselfishness all year round, and then when Mother's Day rolls around, they think "finally, a day for me." They inevitably fall into the trap of trying to make up for a year's worth of self-denial in a single day. You can see how that math wouldn't work, right? Naturally, it's not going to be enough, even if your family throws you a parade down Main Street and gets the two not-dead Beatles back together to serenade you. So you need to treat yourself to the things you want throughout the year. It's almost like what they say about sex: If you know how to please yourself, your partner will know how to please you (actually, they say *pleasure* yourself, but that is the grossest verb ever). Likewise, if you treat yourself to a massage or a nice bottle of perfume once in a while, you'll be less likely to make everything hinge on gifts. Plus, your family will actually start to get an idea of what you like. Your next lingerie gift will be a Dominatrix suit and whip!

Liking Your Kids' Friends and Their Parents

So, today is the day of your son's big play date with two of his kindergarten friends, twin brothers Luke and Ryder, whom you've secretly dubbed "Puke and Biter." You don't normally make a habit of mocking five-year-olds— really! You don't!—but it just so happens that their trendy little names rhyme so nicely with their defining personality traits. Also, the two of them are just about the least likeable, brattiest humans you have ever encountered.

They constantly steal your son's toys and try to eat them (they literally try to eat everything, like puppies with pica). And their mom doesn't stop them, because she says she "doesn't want to shame them into having weird food issues." Brilliant! So instead, they have weird nonfood issues, and you get to watch as Puke and Biter try to chew up your son's G. I. Joe.

But this is only the tip of the iceberg. These kids are also arrogant little know-it-alls (they provided your son with some highly inaccurate, downright creepy information about the facts of life, involving monsters jumping out of the potty), they're hostile (when you hold up your hand for a "high five," Puke punches it), and they're quite possibly the most germ-ridden creatures you have ever met.

And then there's the mom. Oh, that woman. Her parenting philosophy is a deranged combination of anxious helicopter hovering and a free-for-all helicopter wreck. In other words, it's okay for them to "express themselves" by mooning passers-by, but anyone who notices or laughs at their display is clearly a creepy sex offender.

Know Your Reasons

Children in our society have a reputation as being precious, innocent, and the symbol of all that is good about the world. You're really not supposed to dislike them. And it's a weird, unpleasant feeling, hating these little people with their baby teeth and their vulnerable little skinned knees. It makes you feel like a jerk, in fact. But you can hardly help how you feel, can you? And the truth is: *It's not always easy to like other people's kids.*

It might be that the kid just seems weird to you, or has a hairy mole, or always smells like anchovies. It might be related to the time she called you "Strawberry Shortcake" after you dared to dye your hair red. Or maybe it's a genuine behavioral problem—teaching your kid the lyrics to Nicki Minaj songs or encouraging her to make fun of a child with a stutter. Try to figure out what you don't like about this kid. If it's just minor unpleasantness—weird habits or appearance, or just something irksome in his dull little eyes—you need to overlook that for now. If the kid is a bully or encouraging bad behavior, then you might need to intervene or even end the friendship. But just make sure you know where you're coming from—you don't want to be one of those control freak moms who doesn't let her kid choose his or her own friends. You can save that for later, when you try to control who your child marries!

Do Your Best with Parents

Unfortunately, our kids and their social connections may force us into proximity with adults we might not necessarily connect with, even if we were allowed to connect using a ten-foot pole. You might try to discard your adult snobberies and see the good in little Johnny's mom, who wears miniskirts made for fifteen-year-olds, but you're only human. Just think of this as an extension of your workday, where you have to interact with people you don't like all day long. And keep in mind that there's got to be a cutoff for parental involvement in play dates . . . is it eight, nine? Whatever. Kids rarely stay lifetime friends with people they meet at five, right? Fingers crossed!

A More Spacious Living Room When You're Hosting the Big Game

Oh, your husband and his big mouth—he went and told all of his friends that the two of you would be hosting the Big Game in your small, small house. Your living room, in particular, is tiny and cramped enough to seem like a shoebox diorama, or a Barbie Dreamhouse overrun by beer-swilling, jersey-wearing Ken dolls. Except unlike Ken, these guys obviously do not have a beige void in their crotch area, since they also have a tendency to scratch said area while belching and screaming at the sports commentators. The point is that they're going to be so closely packed into your Dreamhouse that they'll be practically falling into the Barbie fireplace. They'll be knocking over the teensy miniature Barbie books on the bookshelf. And as for Barbie—um, I mean you— you'll be squeezed into the corner of the room with your tray of teeny tiny snack foods while your poorly supported doll head partly tips over into the Barbie ironing board.

Okay, so maybe that's an exaggeration, but your living room is small. It's so small that there's only room for a very little bit of living. Time to fake it so you can live large!

Clear the Floor

According to *www.handyamerican.com*, one of the first things you can do to make your living room seem bigger is to get as much stuff off your floor as possible. Take any clutter that might be eating up space and stow it away in boxes. The more your guests can see of the floor, the more "open" the room will look. An open-looking room is going to seem more spacious. Even statues or plants that might be on the floor should be moved up onto shelves to create more floor space. Writers at *www .freshome.com* suggest removing large rugs to make the floor look more spacious. You're going to have to stop your husband from buying that ridiculous "football field area rug" with the yardage markers—you defi- nitely don't want guests to be able to measure your living room in yards.

Keep It Light and Small

Writers at *www.handyamerican.com* say your décor also plays a role in making your living room look bigger (or smaller). Light, neutral, or bright paint colors tend to make a room look larger—be sure to go with solid colors. Dark colors are not a good idea, since they tend to create that overly cozy, borderline "claustrophobically trapped" look. Patterned wallpaper is also considered a no-no for small rooms.

You should also use furniture that is made to scale for small rooms. Just like the Barbie Dreamhouse utilizes teensy furniture, you should choose small furniture for your small living room. Not quite Barbie small, but as small as can comfortably fit an average human. It's also useful to find any kind of furniture that serves a dual function, such as a cabinet that doubles as a coffee table or a sofa bed that also has storage compartments.

Smoke and Mirrors

Who has the best fake-spacious living room of them all? Quite possibly you, if you put a big, Wicked Queen–style mirror on your wall. Writers at *www.handyamerican.com* say a large wall mirror can go a long way toward artificially expanding a small room. Such a mirror is even more effective if you hang it across from something really open and infinite looking, like a fireplace or a window. This will add a sort of endless beauty to the room. Note: Do *not* put the mirror across from your plasma TV with those silly men running around in their tight pants and helmets. That will just create the illusion of endless stupidity. Which is the stupidest sport of them all?? We already have the answer.

Having Fun on a Family Vacation

Oh, boy . . . here you are, at your family reunion in Disney World! Lucky, lucky! In addition to being assaulted by sappy cartoonish schlock at every turn, being fondled by giant mice and ducks, and having that "It's a Small World" song echo through your brain like a mini-stroke, you get to see your long lost extended family! Yay!

There they are, big as life, traipsing around happily in their mouse ears—aunts, uncles, cousins, nieces, nephews, and possibly a few inbred combinations of the above (it is a *very* small world, as it turns out). Oh, look, there's Goofy, with his two teeth and his oversize clown shoes—oh, wait, no, that's your cousin Raymond.

To say that this is not your dream vacation would be like saying that the sun is a little bit warm. You and your husband have thrown away valuable vacation time in order to endure this cornucopia of awkwardness and forced jollity. If you had to break it down, this trip would be 95 percent obligation, 5 percent vacation, or what *www.urbandictionary.com* aptly calls, an "oblication."

The one thing that qualifies this as a vacation—the gorgeous weather— is beside the point, since it's June, and the weather is warm everywhere. Cousin Raymond is jumping up and down, urging you to go with him on the Flight of the Hippogriff ride at the Wizarding World of Harry Potter theme park. You're going to need some serious "magic" to get you through this!

Oblication: Accept It for What It Is

If your trip happens to be an oblication, the first step you can take is to come to terms with this. Yes, you can rail against the fact that you spent vacation time on this, but how will that help you? Instead of thinking of this as a vacation that's being destroyed by annoying family members, think of it as a family obligation that happens to include palm trees. Not to mention nice restaurants, potentially fun rides, and those extra fluffy hotel pillows! If possible, try to find some small way to treat yourself: Order room service at the hotel, or escape with your husband briefly to visit the beach or have margaritas at an outdoor bar. And if you can't manage this, enjoy the people-watching for all it's worth. Just your family alone will provide days of intriguing case study!

Remember: No Vacation Is Perfect

Think back to the many vacations you've had in your life. Some were better than others, certainly, but were any of them *perfect*? Doubtful. That's because we are humans, and humans are not perfect; therefore, human vacations cannot be perfect. Either your luggage got lost and didn't show up until the day you were leaving, or your husband had that nasty sinus infection and you were stuck watching him irrigate his nose all week, or maybe your kid got sunburned and you had to stay in applying aloe.

Or maybe you just couldn't relax. Maybe you kept thinking of that project at work and whether your coworkers would do okay without you. Maybe you felt guilty about how much you ate and ended up spending half of your day in the gym working it off. Or maybe your partner was the one preoccupied, and you were annoyed that he couldn't just be present in the moment. Do you see where I'm going? You might be able to unpack your bags on vacation, but you never really get to unload your baggage. So oftentimes, the same issues that haunted you back home come along for the trip.

This might sound very glass-half-empty, but it really isn't. It's about accepting the limitations of vacation, and therefore taking the pressure off yourself to "achieve" a great vacation. We're all nuts, and our vacations will always be a little bit messed up. It's okay. Hopefully, you can at least have a few pleasant memories. And you'll have your mouse ears to show for it.

Having an Injury to Get Out of Doing Chores

Sometimes, it's a very fine line between "superwoman" and "crazy woman," and my friend, you are teetering precariously on that line. You work a full-time job, volunteer as a coach for your daughter's soccer team, cook nutritious meals for your family, and try to maintain meaningful friendships and a happy marriage. You also pay bills, do grocery shopping, make doctor's appointments, dispense multivitamins, pack lunches, and review homework assignments. You load the dishwasher, load the washing machine, and load the kids into the minivan. In exchange for all of this, your husband says things like, "You're the best, hon," and your kids say, "Bye, Mom!"

You're beginning to suspect that if you have to do *one more thing* without taking a break, you're going to become one of those news headline moms who go berserk and dump their entire family down a trash chute (yet another chore!). It's Friday, and you're not about to spring clean the house this weekend. Faking an injury is actually the lesser of several possible evils. It's time to get hurt!

Trip over a Kids' Toy

One great way to opt out of doing household chores while totally mess-ing with your family's minds is to trip over a kids' toy. You can be busily trying to straighten up the living room and whoops! Down you go, after slipping on a toy truck or a rubber ball or a bunch of teeny tiny plastic parts that go with—what, exactly? Listen—don't worry about that right now; today, those plastic parts are your salvation. Just slip or trip or find some way to cause that item to take you down to the ground. Ouch! Your kids will wish they'd picked up their toys after you'd asked them for the umpteenth time!

If you can't quite bring yourself to guilt your kids, then slip and fall over your husband's shoes that he carelessly left in the middle of the floor, or maybe his duffel bag or—worst of all, his empty bag of Doritos. Those things are slippery!

Once your family discovers that you were injured because of them, they will feel so terrible that they will accept the fact that you are incapaci-tated and can no longer wait on them hand and foot. They will bring you hot tea and let you single-handedly control the remote. Sure, in a couple of days, their annoyance at having to actually do things will override their guilt, but enjoy it while it lasts.

Throw Out Your Back

One of the best injuries you can incur is the old "thrown out back." I've never been entirely clear what "thrown out" means medically, but in my world, when something has been thrown out, it's garbage. That's what your back will be. If you have a useless trash-back, just kick it to the curb and tell your family that you absolutely cannot do chores. Most household chores tend to involve bending down of some kind, so with a no-good back, you're pretty much off the hook. Say you're in a lot of pain and need to lie down and drink a lot of whiskey to dull the agony. Say that you also happen to need to watch *Project Runway*.

A Sling Adds Authenticity

Maybe you've already done the "thrown out back" thing to death, and it's time to come up with a new injury. I would suggest an arm injury, such as a sprained or broken arm or a dislocated elbow. Do not say you have *tennis elbow,* since that makes it sound like you hurt yourself playing a lei-surely game of pairs at the country club. You should accent an arm injury by going to a medical supply store and buying a sling or brace. Keep these items on hand for any time you absolutely cannot do another thing around the house. Aw, and look, your husband is signing your sling! What a sweetheart! Oh, wait. He's actually writing a grocery list on there for you. Sorry—guess you'd better get going!

A Doctor's Note for Your Kids When They Need to Finish a School Project

You basically forced your kids to accompany you on a weekend road trip to see your annoying Great Aunt Josephine, who has been pester-ing you for a visit for months now. Finally, she laid down the law by say-ing, "If I don't even remember what your kids look like, how will I know who to will all that money to?" Touché, Aunt Josie. Message received and understood.

Your kids came along for the visit and endured Aunt Josephine's smothering kisses like sweet little lambs. Maybe they realized how important it was to you. Yeah, right. Actually, they both had looming school projects due and were more than happy for the chance to avoid working on them.

Now, however, it's late Sunday afternoon, the projects are due Monday, and you sort of owe them one. Your kids are going to need to take a sick day to finish their assignments. This is one of those situations where hopefully, you followed your mother's wise advice and married a doctor. If you did the right thing and listened to mom, you can just have your husband scribble off an illegible doctor's note.

If, for some reason, you failed to marry a doctor, what's up with that? As you scramble to fake a doctor's note for your kids, you should take some time and reflect on how you went so terribly wrong.

Stockpile Your Doctor's Stationery

Since doctors' handwriting is well known to be indecipherable nonsense, the main source of credibility for a doctor's note is the stationery. That's why every time you visit the family doc, you should attempt to swipe a few pages off his or her stationery pad. They usually keep this behind their desks in their office. You can either wander into this office by "accident," or if you're brought in the office for a chat, feign lightheadedness and ask if you can sit in the office for a few minutes until you feel better. Once the doc leaves, swipe as many pages of stationery as you can. Once you have the legitimacy of doctors' stationery, you can scrawl just about any old thing you want under it.

The Internet

As you might have guessed, the good old world wide web has also jumped into the fake doctors' note action. In addition to services specifically advertised to create real-looking docs' notes, some sites also appear to sell personalized doctors' stationery. I would proceed with caution on this since it will be very embarrassing for your kids if they get caught. Ultimately, though, it will be most embarrassing for you, the mom who bought a doctor's note off the Internet. You will be the scourge of the community, ostracized, a scarlet letter "www." imprinted on your sick little head. Just saying.

Fake a Veterinarian's Note

You could always take this in a direction no one is expecting by faking a veterinarian's note. Just think about it: If you have a family dog, you can forge a vet's note about the dog's having devoured your child's homework. Be sure to include a full report of the x-ray of the dog's stomach. "The imaging tests of the stomach lining we performed on Tuffy distinctly showed what appears to be an insightful, detailed and well-written report on the stages of cell division. While we were concerned about the volume of paper in Tuffy's digestive tract, we were quite impressed with Kyle's grasp of the nuances of mitosis. We would totally give this an A minus. The minus is only because it is ultimately going to turn into dog excrement. Kudos, Kyle!"

A Busy Schedule to Get Out of Helping at Fundraisers, Meetings, and Family Events

When you were pregnant with your first child, there were the things everyone warned you about—saying goodbye to a full night's sleep, being oblivious to new books, movies, and music for about five years, and never having a complete conversation that didn't include nonsense words. They warned you about the struggle to lose baby weight. They warned you about male babies' tendency to pee dangerously close to your face.

They warned you that while you were pregnant, people might feel entitled to walk right up and touch your stomach, as if your body were somehow community property. And yes—creepily enough, that did happen.

What they didn't warn you about is that even once your kid is out, a mom is *still* community property. Not in the stomach-touching way, but in the bake sale/PTA meeting/soccer carpool/room mother kind of way. Especially once your child enters school and the community at large, the "community" can easily consume you. There are countless community groups that try to tear off pieces of you until you are utterly ripped to pieces and digested. And if you don't let yourself be politely drawn and quartered by the über moms in your community, how much do you really love your kids?

Use Your Phone

It's very likely that these ladies have caught you by phone at least once or twice, maybe as part of a "phone tree" or some absurdly friendly mom contrivance that forces you to make calls for them. Well, show them that you *really* know how to use the phone. Take "important business calls" at the bake sale, argue with your colleagues about the upcoming merger at the PTA meeting, or book a flight to Kuala Lumpur for an upcoming convention at the Sunday school fundraiser. It doesn't necessarily matter if these calls are real; they can be from a friend posing as a work call. But just take them, take a lot of them, and give them priority over the activity at hand. I know, this type of person with the "important cell phone call" is annoying, but that's the whole idea. If you present yourself as that creepy career mom at the bake sale with more of a Bluetooth than a sweet tooth, they most likely won't have you back. Note: One time you don't want to act like a distracted yuppie is when your kid is actually involved. In other words, don't negotiate the terms of a business acquisition as your child performs his oboe solo.

Do Something Occasionally

Although you definitely want to turn down most offers for community involvement due to your incredibly busy schedule, you also don't want to be one of "those women" who is shunned by your community. Sadly, communities—especially small suburban ones—can really be brutal to their outcasts. If you are too aloof and too uninvolved, the bad sentiment toward you might trickle down to your kid. It's not fair, but you might have to occasionally put in an appearance so your kid doesn't suffer. Be sure to choose an event that you might possibly find tolerable, and show up with a smile on your face.

You might think this erratic participation will hurt you, but I beg to differ. Think about the guys you dated when you were younger. Who was the guy that you were most hung up on? Was it the guy who never

ever called you after the first date? Or was it the guy who called you occasionally, then ignored you, then reappeared and called you out of the blue? I'm betting it was that second guy. This is called "intermittent reinforcement," and it's an actual thing. It's used in dog training and slot machines. People keep feeding money into a slot machine based on very occasional, random payouts. That's like what you'll be—an occasional, random payout. Jackpot!

Having a Good Reputation Growing Up

So, rumor has it you had a few wild years when you were younger. Well, so what? Who hasn't done shots of absinthe while eating hallucinogenic mushrooms on an upside down log flume ride? And then there were the nights you *really* got crazy!

You wouldn't necessarily erase your past, even if you have the chance; your crazy history is what made you who you are today—even if who you are today is a person who has extended flashbacks every time you see stagnant water or logs.

The only problem is now you are a mom. As a mom, you tend to want to be a role model and not in the steroid-addled, overly aggressive athlete sense. You truly want to set a good example for your children. After all, you learned all these lessons the hard way, so you want them to learn them the easy way—by avoiding your mistakes.

Whoa, stop right there, Mom. You are living on *Fantasy Island* if you think your kids won't need to make their own mistakes. You can't pass down wisdom—it has to be acquired. You can, however, pass down lip herpes—so let's hope you didn't get that from your days as a tour bus groupie with a trombone band. Ick.

Look, your kids will soon come to realize that you're not perfect and you never were. You can, however, gloss over some of the gorier details, for your sake and theirs.

Post Your Nerdiest Pictures on Facebook

On those Facebook "picture from the past" days, most people seize the opportunity to post photographs that serve as proof that they were once young, thin, and smoking hot. Some people, in fact, sort of "forget" to take down the old high school profile photo, and everyone thinks they are an extremely grainy, faded seventeen-year-old. But that's not going to be your MO. You want to take the most awkward photo from your past, preferably before your red-hot days of rebellion, and put it up. Got one with a bad haircut on full display? Post it! Pics evidencing the "awkward years" when you were still growing into your outsize hips and thighs like a puppy with gigantic paws? Up it goes! Wraparound sunglasses? Post it! Pink braces? Hell, yes! When everyone sees what a nerd you were, no one will ever think you got into trouble. Trouble wouldn't touch *you* with a ten-foot pole!

Make a Deal with Your Closet Skeletons

In the event that you live in the same general area where you grew up, you may encounter parents who once shared some of your youthful antics. Even worse, their big-mouthed kids may encounter your kids. What you need to do is come to an "understanding" with these skeletons in your closet. First, you can sweetly and casually say to them, "We don't need to rehash that old stuff in front of the kids, do we?" Most likely, they will be just as eager to forget that stuff as you are. If not, you may have to break out some threats. Surely, if this person knows a little bit about your past, you know a bit about theirs, too. Simply dangle a scandalous tidbit from their days of yore in front of them, and indicate that you will tell your kid, who will tell their kid, if they don't shut down the rumor mill immediately. Yes, the closure of the rumor mill might put them and several others out of a job, but they can always open up a Jerk Store or something. That would keep everyone in your town employed for a nice long time.

If it comes down to it, and your kids confront you on something you did years ago, you can just tell them that you are human and that you have made mistakes. But just because you secretly cooked meth in home economics class doesn't mean they are allowed to do it!

Having Fun to Get Your Kid to a Doctor's Appointment or on a Shopping Trip

Lucky you—it's the day of your two-year-old's annual pediatrician appointment. The first year, she didn't really put up much of a fight going to the doctor's, since she was mostly busy being an amorphous blob. As difficult as babies are in terms of waking you up in the night and not adhering to civilized bathroom etiquette, they are just awesome about going places. A baby won't subject you to a lengthy interrogation about where you're going when you put them in the car. They won't even ask, "Hey, Ma, where are we headed?" They'll just gurgle and make a giant mess in their diapers. Look, every age is a tradeoff.

Now, though, she's *way* beyond being loaded into the minivan like a frolicsome dog that always assumes he's going to a happy farm where milk bones grow on trees. She screws up her little face in outright suspicion, and asks, like a stoic little hostage, "Where are you taking me?"

But you can see trouble brewing beneath her cool gaze. She's now old enough to associate *doctor* with needles, gagging tongue sticks, and rubber hammer abuse. She knows full well that the lame little lollipop she gets at the end isn't nearly enough to cover the suffering she'll endure. It's probably not a smart idea to lie outright, since when she gets to the doctor's instead of the zoo, she will pitch a fit.

Pull a "Life Is Beautiful"

Parents: if you haven't seen the 1997 movie *Life Is Beautiful*, you should check it out, if only as a parenting guide. In this poignant, tragicomic film, Roberto Benigni's character convinces his four-year-old son that their experience living in a concentration camp is "just a game." Players try to earn "points," and the first person to earn 1,000 points wins a tank. Kids who cry or scream or complain about being hungry lose points; quiet kids who avoid the Nazi guards win points. This superdad maintains this illusion all the way through the film, right up until an American tank comes to free the camp (epic winning!). My point is, if this dad can make a concentration camp fun, don't you think you can manage to make a one-hour pediatrician's appointment fun? I mean, *come on*, Mom! Are you going to let yourself be outdone by a *movie dad*? Tell your kid she's in competition with the other kids in the office—the kid who is quietest, most brave, and least freaked out wins a toy. Of course, if she behaves, this means you will have to buy her a toy afterward. If not, maybe she'll compete harder next time!

Trouble First, Treat Later

A more conventional system for coaxing your child into that minivan is the promise of a treat after the troublesome ordeal. If you're taking your child on a dull shopping trip, tell your child that you'll take her for ice cream afterward. In the case of a dreaded doctor's appointment, maybe a picnic in the park would be a good motivator. It's a very straightforward delay-of-gratification approach. If the child endures the horrible doctor's appointment or the vexing trip to Whole Foods, she will get to have something fun afterward (provided she doesn't go on a shelf-sweeping, cart-tipping, doctor-punching rampage).

Another great modern tool is the car DVD player. If you have one of these, just pop in your child's favorite movie or even one she hasn't yet seen. This will keep her riveted on the way there and rewarded on the way home. Just imagine if your poor mom had been able to placate you with a movie on the way to the doctor's—she wouldn't have had to keep threatening, "I will pull this car over right now!" and "Wait until I tell your father!" Instead, she just would have said, "If you sit too close to that TV, you will go blind!" And off you would go to your much needed eye doctor's appointment!

Acknowledgments

I never would have been able to fake knowing all the stuff in this book if it weren't for certain people.

Thanks to Adams Media, particularly Diane Garcia, for giving me this endlessly fun opportunity. I've enjoyed every minute of writing this book—no faking required.

Thanks to my supportive, loving and crazy family. Love all of yous.

Thanks to all of my wonderful friends, I love you all.

Thanks to my fake kids who are actually cats. You didn't really do anything, but you looked cute.

Most of all, I thank Dave Mullin, for giving me the confidence to fake being able to write. I know I owe you everything—one day I'll pay up.

About the Author

Jennifer Byrne writes humor, fiction, and journalism. Her writing has appeared in *McSweeney's Internet Tendency*, *mental_floss*, *Opium*, *The Rumpus*, USAToday.com, the *Philadelphia Inquirer*, *PopMatters*, and more. She was a finalist for the Robert Benchley Humor Prize. She lives in Glassboro, New Jersey.